Long Circular Walks Western Hertfordshire
by John N. Merrill

Maps, pencil sketches and photographs by John N. Merrill

"I hike the paths and trails of the world for others to enjoy."

THE JOHN MERRILL FOUNDATION

The Long Circular Walks Series.

2009

THE JOHN MERRILL FOUNDATION
32, Holmesdale, Waltham Cross, Hertfordshire, England. EN8 8QY

Tel/Fax - 01992-762776
E-mail - marathonhiker@aol.com
www. johnmerrillwalkguides.com

A catalogue record for this book is available from the British Library.

Typset and designed by *The John Merrill Foundation*
Printed and handmade by *John N. Merrill.*
Book layout and cover design by *John N. Merrill*

©Text, maps, sktches, photographs and routes - John N. Merrill, HonMUniv, 2007.

ISBN 978 -0-9556511-1-3
First published - October 2007.
Special limited edition.

Typeset in Humanst521 - bold, italic, and plain 11pt, 14pt and 18pt
Main titles in 18pt .**Humanst521 Bd BT** by John Merrill in
Adobe Pagemaker on a Apple Macintosh.

Please note - *The maps in this guide are purely illustrative. You are encouraged to use the appropriate 1:25,000 O.S. Explorer map as detailed on each walk.*

John Merrill has walked all the routes in this book and detailed what he found. Meticulous research has been undertaken to ensure that this publication is highly accurate at the time of going to press. The publishers, however, cannot be held responsible for alterations, errors, omissions, or for changes in details given. They would welcome information to help keep the book up to date.

Cover photographs by John N. Merrill
© The John Merrill Foundation 2007.

 Printed on 100% recycled paper

The author on Tower Bridge, after completing
Walk for Life, a charity walk in June 2008.

About the author.

Over the last 38 years John Merrill has walked over 190,000 miles, wearing out 106 pairs of boots in the process. He has completed a remarkable number of marathon walks - walking more than 28 miles per day on average - including being the first person to walk around Britain - 7,000 miles - in ten months. He has walked across Europe, India, Nepal, Asia, America, and along the great trails of America and Canada. He has completed many Pilgrim routes to Santiago de Compostela, Canterbury, Walsingham and Trondheim in Norway. Many more marathons are planned.

He has written more than 300 guidebooks to his walks, most of which he prints and publishes himself. After his coast walk he realised the fame game prevented his from doing what he was destined to do, and that was to simply walk and write. He purposefully left the stage and concentrated on what he wanted to do. He does not consult anyone, promote or seek publicity; preferring to follow his own quiet spiritual path through life. This means he can write a book, on average one every month. He is not beholden to anyone, just a free spirit, with no staff, agents or editors. As a result he is not rich in money terms but in life and places walked to, a millionaire.

He is not a loner, quite the reverse, but to get the material and accomplish his walks - he who travels alone, travels fastest. And, by going alone you never forget. He is guided and has a very deep spiritual faith and has never come to any harm or put a foot wrong. The only way to be close to nature and see its huge variety is by walking; no other sport/exercise gives you that connectedness to the earth. He does no research beforehand, preferring to walk around the corner and come to a church, historic house, sacred site etc., and discover for himself their secrets. To be aware of what's next is to dampen the impact.

"A journey of a thousand miles, begins with a single step."
Lao Tzu (The Tao Te Ching).

I am on a long journey, which continues daily - one life is not enough.

> "Do not seek fame.
> Do not make plans.
> Do not be absorbed by activities.
> Do not think that you know.
> Be aware of all that is and dwell in the infinite.
> Wander where there is no path.
> Be all that heaven gave you, but act as though
> you have received nothing.
> Be empty, that is all."
>
> Chuang Tzu

Contents

The River Ver and Shafford Mill, near St. Albans - see Nomansland walk, page 38.

INTRODUCTION

My journey through Hertfordshire continues, this time exploring the western side half of the county. Being more built up the walks are more spread out, but combined they explore the area fully. There are some amazing places off the beaten track, which I am sure will astound you and are equal to anything. The county may not have hills, but it does have tranquil rivers, a meandering canal, many historical buildings and most attractive villages, steeped in history.

I began with a walk right around Welwyn Garden City, before heading north to Nomansland Common - what a gem that is. Then on along the Rivers Lee and Colne, before walking along the Grand Union Canal in Hemel Hempstead, Watford and Rickmansworth. The latter was fascinating and linked with the River Chess, a most picturesque valley. To complete the story I headed far west to Ashwell, probably the finest village in Hertfordshire. My journey ended near Stevenage, around the Knebworth area.

I am sad my journey is over and in the two long walk books, I covered some 400 miles. A walk should be a journey of discovery and wonder, so lace your boots on and set off on one them. I am sure, like me, you will be impressed at what the county has to offer. May the sun shine all day and the rain fall only evening when you have finished!

Happy walking

Alan W Mennell

7

ABOUT THE WALKS
- some general comments.

Whilst every care is taken detailing and describing the walks in this book, it should be borne in mind that the countryside changes by the seasons and the work of man. I have described the walk to the best of my ability, detailing what I have found actually on the walk in the way of stiles and signs. You should always walk with the appropriate O.S. map, as detailed for each walk, open on the walk area for constant reference. Obviously with the passage of time stiles become broken or replaced by a ladder stile, a small gate or a kissing gate. Signs too have a habit of being broken or pushed over - vandelism. All the route follow rights of way and only on rare occasions will you have to overcome obstacles in its path, such as a blown down tree, barbed wire fence or an electric fence. On rare occasions rights of way are rerouted and these ammendments are included in the next edition. Inns have a frustrating habit of changing their name, then back to the original one!

All rights of way have colour coded arrows; on marker posts, stiles/gates and trees; these help you to show the direction of the right of way -

Yellow - Public footpath.
Blue - Public bridleway.
Red - Byway open to all traffic (BOAT).
Black - Road used as a public path (RUPP).
White - Concessionary and Permissive path

The seasons bring occasional problems whilst out walking which should also be borne in mind. In the height of summer paths become overgrown and you may have to fight your way through in a few places. In low lying areas the fields are often full of crops, and although the pathline goes straight across it may be more practical to walk round the field edge to get to the next stile or gate. In summer the ground is generally dry but in autumn and winter, especially because of our climate, the surface can be decidedly wet and slippery; sometimes even gluttonous mud!

These comments are part of countryside walking which help to make your walk more interesting or briefly frustrating. Standing in a track up to your ankles in mud might not be funny at the time but upon reflection was one of the highlights of the walk!

The mileage for each section is based on three calculations -

1. pedometer and stepometer readings.
2. the route map measured on the map.
3. the time I took for the walk.

I believe the figure stated for each section to be very accurate but we all walk differently and not always in a straight line! The time allowed for each section is on the generous side and does not include pub stops etc. The figure is based on the fact that on average a person walks 2 1/2 miles an hours but less in hilly terrain. Allow 20 minutes to walk a mile; ten minutes for 1/2 mile and five minutes for 1/4 mile. On average you will walk 2,000 strides to a mile - an average stride is 31 inches..

"For every mile you walk, you extend your life by 21 minutes"

The Art of Walking the John Merrill Way.

1. Always set off in the clothes you plan to wear all day, given the weather conditions. Only on sudden changes in the weather will I stop and put on a waterproof or warmer clothing.

2. Set off at a steady comfortable pace, which you can maintain all day. You should end the walk as fresh as when as you started.

3. Maintain your pace and don't stop. Stopping for any period of time disrupts your rhythm and takes upwards of a mile to settle back down into the flow/ease of movement.

4. Switch off your mobile phone and music centre, and listen and enjoy the countryside - the smells of the flowers, bird song, the rustle of the leaves and the tinkling stream.

5. Ignore the mileage and ascents - don't tick off the miles, just concentrate on what the walk's goal is. To think otherwise slows you down and makes the walk a struggle rather than a joy. In a similar vein, when ascending just keep a steady pace and keep going. To stop is to disrupt the flow and make the ascent interminable.

6. Whilst a walk is a challenge to complete, it is not just exercise. You should enjoy the world around you; the flowers, birds, wildlife and nature and look at and explore the historical buildings and church's that you pass. All are part of life's rich tapestry.

7. Remember that for every mile that you walk, you extend your life by 21 minutes.

8. A journey of a 1,000 miles begins with a single step and a mile requires 2,000 strides.

"The expert traveller
leaves no footprints."
Lao Tzu.

Follow the Countryside Code.

* Be safe - plan ahead
and follow any signs.

* Leave gates and property
as you find them.

* Protect plants and animals, and take
your litter home.

* Keep dogs
under close control.

* Consider
other people.

EQUIPMENT NOTES
.....some personal thoughts from John N. Merrill

Today there is a bewildering variety of walking gear, much is superfluous to general walking in Britain. As a basic observation, people over dress for the outdoors. Basically equipment should be serviceable and do the task. I don't approve of or use walking poles; humans were built to walk with two legs! The following are some of my throughts gathered from my walking experiences.

BOOTS - For summer use and day walking I wear lightweight boots. For high mountains and longer trips I prefer a good quality boot with a full leather upper, of medium weight, with a vibram sole. I always add a foam cushioned insole to help cushion the base of my feet. Contary to popular belief, I do not use nor recommend Merrell footwear!

SOCKS - I generally wear two thick pairs as this helps minimise blisters. The inner pair are of loop stitch variety and approximately 80% wool. The outer are a thick rib pair of approximately 80% wool.

CLOTHES & WATERPROOFS - for general walking I wear a T shirt or cotton shirt with a cotton wind jacket on top, and shorts - even in snow! You generate heat as you walk and I prefer to layer my clothes to avoid getting too hot. Depending on the season will dictate how many layers you wear. In soft rain I just use my wind jacket for I know it quickly dries out. In heavy or consistant rain I slip on a poncho, which covers my pack and allows air to circulate, while keeping dry. Only in extreme conditions will I don overtrousers, much preferring to get wet and feel comfortable. I never wear gaiters, except when cross country skiing, in snow and glacier crossings.

FOOD - as I walk I carry bars of chocolate, for they provide instant energy and are light to carry. In winter a flask of hot coffee is welcome. I never carry water and find no hardship from not doing so, but this is a personal matter! From experience I find the more I drink the more I want and sweat. You should always carry some extra food such as trail mix & candy bars etc., for emergencies.

RUCKSACKS - for day walking I use a climbing rucksack of about 30/40 litre capacity and although it leaves excess space it does mean that the sac is well padded, with an internal frame and padded shoulder straps. Inside apart from the basics for one day, in winter I carry gloves, wear a hat and carry a spare pullover and a pair of socks.

MAP & COMPASS - when I am walking I always have the relevant map - preferably 1:25,000 scale - open in my hand. This enables me to constantly check that I am walking the right way. In case of bad weather I carry a compass, which once mastered gives you complete confidence in thick cloud or mist - you should always know where you are.

11

AROUND WELWYN GARDEN CITY
- 19 MILES - *East Map*

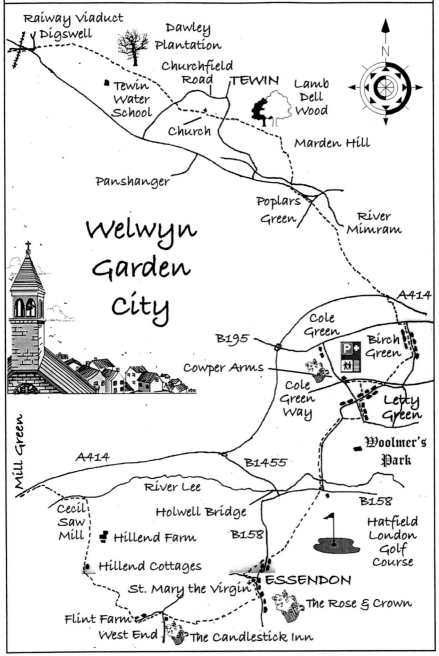

Raiway Viaduct
Digswell

Dawley
Plantation

Churchfield
Road

TEWIN

Lamb
Dell
Wood

N

Tewin
Water
School

Church

Marden Hill

Panshanger

Poplars
Green

River
Mimram

Welwyn
Garden
City

A414

Cole
Green

B195

Birch
Green

P

Cowper Arms

Cole
Green
Way

Letty
Green

Woolmer's
Park

Mill Green

A414

B1455

B158

River Lee

Cecil
Saw
Mill

Holwell Bridge

Hatfield
London
Golf
Course

Hillend Farm

B158

Hillend Cottages

St. Mary the Virgin

ESSENDON

The Rose & Crown

Flint Farm

West End

The Candlestick Inn

AROUND WELWYN GARDEN CITY
- 19 MILES
- allow 7 to 8 hours.

Basic route - Cole Green Way Car Park - Letty Green - B158 - Essendon - West End - Flint Farm - Hillend Cottages - Lea Valley Walk - Cecil Saw Mill - A414 - Mill Green - Woodhall Farm - Stanborough Park - A1M - Lemsford - Brocket Hall - Waterend - Ayot Greenway - Ayot St. Peter - White Hill - Welwyn - Digswell - Trewin Church - Lamb Dell Wood - River Mimram - Poplars Green - Brocket Hill - Chain Walk - A414 - Birch Green - Cole Green Way Car Park.

Map - O.S. 1:25,000 Explorer Series No. 182 - St. Albans & Hatfield.

Car park and start - Cole Green Way Car Park, near Cowper Arms, Labby Green. Grid Ref. 285112.

Inns - Cowper Arms, Labby Green at entrance to car park. The Rose & Crown, Essendon. The Candlestick Inn, West End. The Green Man, Mill Green. The Sun Inn, Lemsford. The Steamer Inn, Welwyn.

Cafe - Beside South Lake, Stanborough Park.

ABOUT THE WALK - The aim is to encircle Welwyn Garden City, not keeping to the city's limits but to the delightful countryside that surrounds it. The southern and first half explores Essendon and the River Lee. En route you pass a working mill, lakes and a stunning hall. At Waterend you leave the Lee and begin the northern half to Ayot St. Peter and onto Welwyn and your last "refreshment" point. For a while you walk near the River Mimram before crossing it at a beautiful picnic area before the final "hill". Walking beside woodland you cross the A414 and walk through Birch Green back to the Cole Green Way. The whole walk is through very pleasant countryside and passes two churches which were rebuilt within a year, one following a fire and the other by Zeppelin bombs.

WALKING INSTRUCTIONS - From the car park, turn left along the Cole Green Way for a hundred yards - you will return along the Way to your right. Reach a path post on the right and turn right along the path to Chapel Lane in Letty Green. Turn right to the former chapel - St. John's on the corner. Turn left beside it along Woolmers Lane. In a short distance, opposite house no. 25, turn right onto a RUPP path. Follow it to the road and turn left along it, soon descending to the River Lee. As you descend to your left can be seen the white painted, Woolmers Park. At the bottom and at the junction with the B158 road, turn right and in a few yards, left at a kissing gate. Follow the wide tarmaced path as it ascends through the Hatfield London Golf Course. In almost 1/2 mile, near the "top", the tarmaced path turns left near pine trees. Turn right and follow another path and then cross a fairway to a path post and onto the Essendon road (B158). Go straight across to another gate and path sign - West End Lane 1/4 mile. The path line keeps to the right of the houses and aim for the top righthand one - The Wheatsheaf, where there is a stile. Turn left passing the house and in a few yards right to pass St. Mary the Virgin church.

Continue ahead and straight ahead along the B158 through the village. In 100 yards opposite Sunset House on the left and before the Rose and Crown Inn, turn right onto a signed path. The path soon descends - steeply - through woodland and onto a footbridge over Essendon Brook. Cross and keep to the righthand side of the field ascending gently to a track. Turn left and in a few yards right at a kissing gate. Keep to the righthand side of the field to a stile and onto the road at West End, with The Candlestick Inn on the left. Cross the road and keep straight ahead on a no through road. Pass Flint Farm on your right and then a row of cottages. Immediately after turn right, as footpath signed, to a stile and follow a hedged track. Follow it as it curves left then right and past pine woodland on the left, as you slowly descend. You have good views to your right, to Welwyn Garden City. Follow the track to a stile and onto the driveway at Hillend Cottages; part of the Hatfield Estate. Follow the drive down past Hillend Farm on your right and onto the River Lee path at the bottom. Follow the road left by the river on your right to a bridge. Cross and pass Cecil Saw Mill on the left. Continue on the road to the A414, Hertford Road.

Cross the busy A414 road, with care. Turn left along along the tarmaced path on its righthand side to Mill Green, with the Green Man Inn on the right.

Keep ahead on the minor no through road to reach the Mill Green Museum and Mill on the right. You are also guided by Lee Valley Walk signs. Follow the road round to the right and onto an ascending path (left) to the main road - A1000. Turn right and pass the entrance to Bush Hall (Kiplings Restaurant) on the left. Soon afterwards on your left follow a minor road at Teaside House, and part way along, turn left along the drive to Woodhall Farm - as Lee Valley Walk arrowed. Follow the tarmaced driveway to Woodhall Farm; the lefthand buildings has a coat of arms and the date 1785? Bear right and follow the path to a railway tunnel. The otherside reach a kissing gate and South Lake of Stanborough Park. Bear left and walk around the lefthand side of the lake to the A6129 road, with the Terranova Restaurant & Cafe on the right.

Walk through road tunnel by the river to North Lake. Walk along its righthand side to its end, with the River Lee on your right. Keep straight ahead to A1M and descend steps to the river and walk through the river tunnel to steps at the other end. The path is prone to flooding in winter, but there are stepping stones! Just after gain a kissing gate and bear right with a fence on your left. Continue on the defined path to stiles and onto the road at Lemsford. Turn right and in a few yards left at Lemsford Mill - just ahead is The Sun Inn. Cross the mill stream and River Lee. Just after the path divides; keep to the righthand one, with woodland on your right. Keep straight ahead on the path to a path junction with tennis courts just ahead. Keep straight ahead on the path now with a golf course on the right and soon Brocket Hall on your left. Keep straight ahead all the time, passing the stable block on the left and then open countryside to a wood. Here the path descends to Hyde Corner. Again keep straight ahead on the defined path past woodland on the left and the River Lee to the road at Waterend, with a ford on your left. Turn right to the impressive Sparrowhall and immediately turn left on a track - still on the Lee Valley Walk. In a few yards, leave it and turn right up steps and follow the path uphill to Sparrowhall Farm on the right. Keep ahead to Sparrowhall Bridge over the former railway line - now the Ayot Greenway. On the other side turn left and follow the path down to the trail. Turn left and pass under the bridge.

Follow the Ayot Greenway for 3/4 mile (15 mins) to the third right of way on the left. Turn left at the stile and keep to the righthand path just inside Saul's Wood, as you curve right to the road at Ayot St. Peter. Turn right to the church and in a few yards on your left is the second path sign - White Hill 1/4 mile. The defined path leads to a stile and on beside a hedge on your right to another stile before the road at White Hill. Turn left passing Whitehill Farm and before the last house on your left, with views, turn right as path signed -

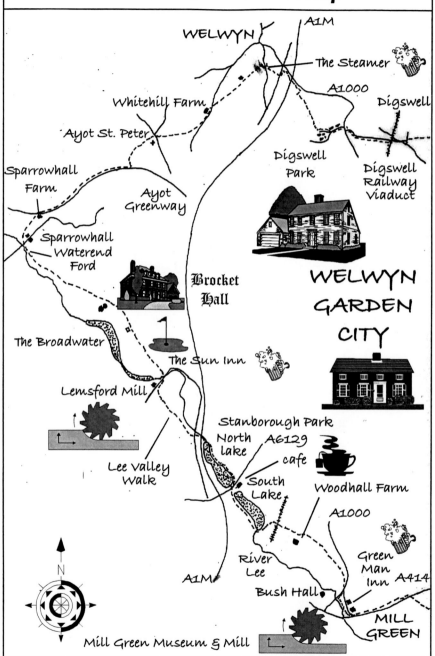

WELWYN

A1M

The Steamer

A1000

Digswell

Whitehill Farm

Ayot St. Peter

Digswell Park

Digswell Railway Viaduct

Sparrowhall Farm

Ayot Greenway

Sparrowhall Waterend Ford

Brocket Hall

WELWYN GARDEN CITY

The Broadwater

The Sun Inn

Lemsford Mill

Stanborough Park

North Lake

A6129

cafe

Lee Valley Walk

South Lake

Woodhall Farm

A1000

River Lee

A1M

Bush Hall

Green Man Inn

A414

N

MILL GREEN

Mill Green Museum & Mill

Welwyn 1/2 mile. Descend the defined path, with views of Welwyn, down the field to a kissing gate with tennis courts on the left. Continue to another kissing gate and lane. Go straight across into a fenced path with a reservoir on your left. Follow the path past St. Mary's school and then straight ahead along Ottway Walk to a road. Turn right and left past The Streamer Inn along Broomsfield Road. In a few yards, turn right, as path signed, and follow the path to the main road (A1000/B197).

Turn left and in a few yards right to the other side of the road to gain a tarmaced path. Follow it parallel to the road, as it descends and turns right and descends to the A1000. Continue ahead passing under the A1M and then through a subway on the right. Follow it under and then left back to the A1000. Continue ahead a few more yards before turning right onto a wide path through woodland. In 100 yards the path turns sharp left, being a fenced and hedged path. Follow it to houses and road. Go straight across and follow a another path to a Cul de sac - Willow Grove. Turn left and walk past the houses to Knightsfield Road. Turn left and follow to the road to the A1000 road. Cross to your right to Digswell Park Road, and follow the "lane" past Digswell Lake on the right and onto the impressive Digswell Railway Viaduct. Pass under and at the road junction, just beyond, cross the road to reach Harmer Green Lane - for Digswell. Turn left passing West Lodge and then right along Bridlepath No. 37 - Tewin 1 1/4 miles.

The bridlepath is well defined with a track and concrete path. In more then 1/4 mile it curves right and onto a kissing gate and path crossroads. Ignore all turnings and keep straight ahead on the bridlepath with Tewin Water (School) on your right. Walk through woodland - Dawley Plantation; more than 1/4 mile later the track bears right and leads to Churchfield Road. Go straight across into Westley Wood, at the end cross a bridleway and keep ahead, aiming for the tower of Tewin church. Walk into the churchyard and aim for the far righthand corner of it, to a kissing gate. Through turn left along the field edge and descend before ascending by the fence on your left to the Tewin road. Go straight across to path sign - Hertford Road 1 mile. The path leads straight ahead to Lamb Dell Wood. Descend steps through it before walking along an avenue of trees to a footpath post, with Marden Hill House on your left. Turn right along the line of oak trees to the end of the field. Turn left and in 100 yards right and descend a wide fenced path to a bridge over the River Mimram. This area is open access land and makes a wonderful stopping place, admidst the attractive meadows and flowing river.

Continue to the road and turn left and follow it to a house at Poplars Green, and road triangle. Turn right and keep straight ahead across the other side road - to Cole Green - to a lodge and path sign - Birch Green 1 1/4 miles. The path, first along a quarry track, then path close to it, leads to a kissing gate and tarmaced road. Cross to another kissing gate and then bear slightly right to a stile and ascend a well defined path through woodland to the top. Continue with the wood on your left for 1/2 mile to a fenced path leading to a green metal footbridge over the A414. Cross over and descend the other side and follow the path to near a house before turning right along the field edge to two stiles before bearing left to the house drive. Follow it to the Cole Green road. Turn left and soon right along the road into Birch Green. Pass the war memorial and Hertingfordbury Cowper Primary School on your left. Follow the path on the righthand side of the road, avoiding the righthand bend in the road, on your left. Here on the right is the final path sign - Chapel Lane 1/4 mile. Follow the path by the houses and then along the field edge and onto the Cole Green Way. Turn right and follow the way back to the car park 1/4 mile away.

COLE GREEN WAY - Former railway line between Welwyn and Hertford built in 1858 and closed in 1966. Made into a pedestrian/cyclist way in 1978.

HERTFORDSHIRE CHAIN WALK - Created by the East Hertfordshire Footpath Society. A chain of fifteen linking circular walks, covering 86 miles, between Crews Hill Station, Enfield and Ashwell & Morden Station, Cambridgeshire.

WOOLMERS PARK - In the 18th. century it was owned by the Duke of Bridgewater. In the 1820's the building was remodelled. Later the owners were the Queen's grandparents, Lord and Lady Strathmore. The Queen and her sister, Margaret, often went to the chapel in Letty Green.

Essendon church.

ESSENDON - The Rose & Crown Inn dates from 1756. The Zeppelin that dropped its last bombs on Essendon, destroying most of the church and several cottages, finally came down in flames at Cuffley. Of the original church only the 15th. century tower remains.

The tablet on the outside church wall records its dramatic history -

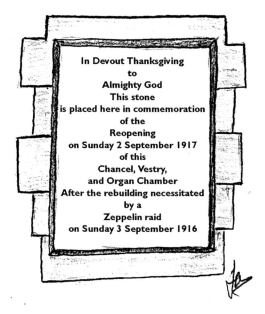

In Devout Thanksgiving
to
Almighty God
This stone
is placed here in commemoration
of the
Reopening
on Sunday 2 September 1917
of this
Chancel, Vestry,
and Organ Chamber
After the rebuilding necessitated
by a
Zeppelin raid
on Sunday 3 September 1916

THE CANDLESTICK INN - Originally known as the Chequers but changed its name to the Candlestick in 1966. It is said that before electricity came to the area, the landlord was a bit of a miser and had only one candle on the bar for the customers to see by. When he had to go to the cellar he took the solitary candle with him, leaving his customers in the dark. Outside is a horse tie bar and is a popular stopping point for horse riders.

LEA VALLEY WALK - 50 mile walk from the source of the River Lee near Luton to Limehouse basin, London. The section from Hertford to Limehouse Basin - 28 miles - is beside the River Lee Navigation. See my River Lee Navigation books for walks on this delightful navigation.

HATFIELD HOUSE - Impressive family home of the Cecil family - Lord Salisbury; here Queen Elizabeth 1st. grew up

MILL GREEN MILL & MUSEUM - The Green Man Inn dates from 1850. The 18th. century mill is open to the public and flour is still ground here for locally made bread.

STANBOROUGH PARK - Opened in 1970 with man made lakes.

LEMSFORD - The mill dates from 1863.

BROCKET HALL - The estate was bought by Sir Mathew Lamb in 1746. In 1760 the fine square red bricked hall was begun, designed by James Paine, and took 20 years to complete. Below over the River Lee can be seen the arched bridge, designed by James Paine and built in 1772-4.

WATER END FARM - Exceptionally fine red bricked building, formerly the Manor House of the Jennings family, built about 1610.

AYOT GREENWAY - Former railway line from Welwyn Garden City to Wheathampstead; now a walking and cycling route.

TEWIN WATER - Large mansion with a west from of seven bays. In 1819 it was described as, "a new and handsome house."

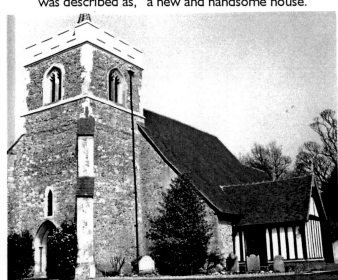

TEWIN CHURCH - Dedicated to St. Peter; parts date back to the 11th. century. The chancel is 13th. century. Inside the porch is a monument to General Joseph Sabine; Governor of Gibraltar, who died in 1739.

WELWYN - although just off the route it is well worth a visit to see St. Mary's church and the many houses closeby, dating back to the 18th. century. Under the A1M is a Roman Bath. The Steamer Inn dates from 1851 and was originally known as the Steam Engine.

DIGSWELL RAILWAY VIADUCT - One the finest architectural achievements of the "Railway Age" and part of the London to Peterborough line, of the Great Northern Railway. Built between 1848-50, spanning 500 feet and 98 feet above the River Mimram. It has 40 brick arches with 30 ft span arches and was designed by Lewis Cubitt and built by Thomas Brassey; it is now a Grade 11 listed structure. On August 25th. 1851, Queen Victoria was on a train to Balmoral but on reaching the viaduct, she refused to cross it. Instead she got off the train and was taken by coach to the otherside - Welwyn North Station, where she reboarded the train!

AYOT ST. PETER - Delightful church built between 1874-5, from red, blue and white brick. The clock has a blue face.

The church stone, on the outside wall, records it's history -

**This stone laid by Earl Cowper K.C.,
April 7th. 1875
Was taken from doorway of the
former church which was stuck by
lightning and burnt July 10th. 1874.**

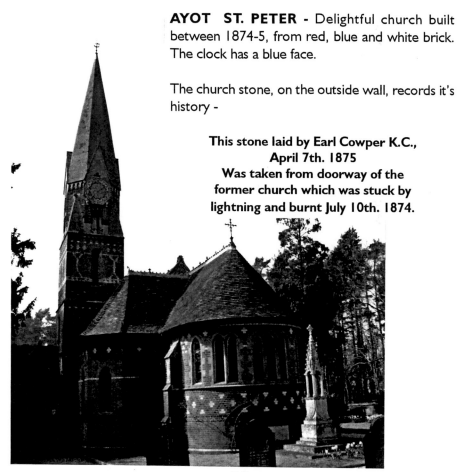

23

NORTON BURY, ASHWELL, CALDECOTE & STOTFOLD - 15 MILES

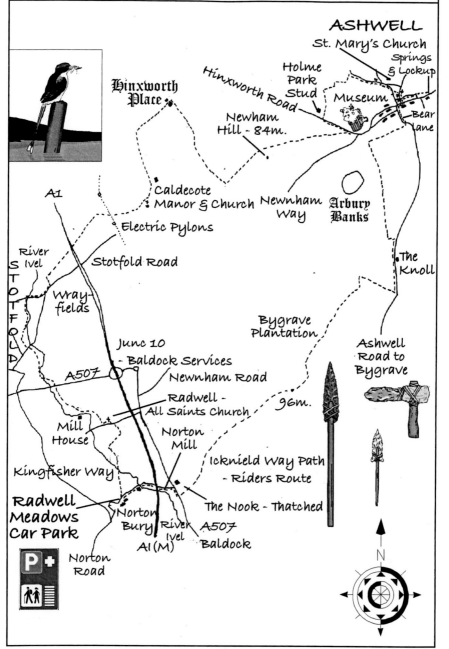

ASHWELL
St. Mary's Church
Springs & Lockup
Holme Park Stud
Museum
Hinxworth Road
Hinxworth Place
Newham Hill - 84m.
Bear Lane

A1
River Ivel
STOTFOLD
Caldecote Manor & Church
Newham Way
Arbury Banks
Electric Pylons
Stotfold Road
The Knoll
Wray-fields
Bygrave Plantation
Junc 10 - Baldock Services
A507
Newham Road
Ashwell Road to Bygrave
Radwell - All Saints Church
96m.
Mill House
Norton Mill
Kingfisher Way
Icknield Way Path - Riders Route
Radwell Meadows Car Park
Norton Bury
River Ivel
A507 Baldock
A1(M)
The Nook - Thatched
Norton Road
N

NORTON BURY, ASHWELL, CALDECOTE & STOTFOLD

- 15 MILES

- allow 6 hours.

Basic route - Radwell Meadows Car Park (Norton Bury) - Norton Mill - A507 - Icknield Way Path - Spot height 96m. - Bygrave Plantation - Ashwell Road - The Knoll - Arbury Banks - Partridge hall - Ashwell - Hinxworth Road - Newnham Hill - Hinxworth Place - Caldecote Manor & Church - A1 - Stotfold - River Ivel - The Kingfisher Way - A507 - Radwell, All Saints Church - Radwell Meadows Car Park.

Map - O.S. 1:25,000 Explorer Series No. 193 - Luton & Stevenage.

Car Park and start - Radwell Meadows car park, Nortonbury Lane, Norton Bury. Just off Norton Road at Grid Ref. 234349.

Inns - Rose & Crown Inn, The Three Tuns and Bushel & Strike in Ashwell. One off the route in Stotfold.

ABOUT THE WALK - A forgotten corner of Hertfordshire, full of history and stunning and extensive views. First you follow a section of the Icknield Way, with 360° views on the way, passing the Iron Age Fort of Arbury banks, before reaching the village of Ashwell. Ashwell is arguably the finest village in Hertfordshire, full of history and architecture, and we wander around to see many of the historic buildings and the springs; the start of the River Rhee. Leaving the village you ascend Newnham Hill with more fine views before descending to the remote and unspoilt Hinxworth Place. Next you reach the remote hamlet of Caldecote with a Manor and aisleless church. Pressing on towards Stotfold and briefly into Bedfordshire, you cross the A1. There is no bridge here, just a split crash barrier on the dual carriageways. Great care is needed to cross this busy road. Gaining the River Ivel near Stotfold, you pick up the Kingfisher Way and follow it south back into Hertfordshire near Radwell and its unspoilt gem of a church. In another mile you are back at Radwell Meadows Car Park.

WALKING INSTRUCTIONS - Starting from the car park, return to the entrance - on your left is your return path. At the road - Nortonbury Lane, turn left and follow it to Norton Mill, complete with high loading doors, and the River Ivel. Continue on the lane following it right and under the A1 (M) and onto the A507 road, opposite the thatched house, The Nook. Turn right and in 100 yards, turn left onto a track - path signed The Icknield Way - Riders Route. At first it is a track/drive to a house and barns 1/4 mile away. Leaving them it is just a track as you begin to ascend gently in open countryside. As you reach the summit plateau you have extensive views to your right. In 1 1/2 miles from the road (30 mins.) you pass the site of the triangulation pillar at 96m; to your right is the hamlet of Bygrave. Just after you have a hedge on your right and soon bear left to a small electric sub station on an electric pole, with a small building below. Continue on the track, now with the hedge on your left, as you begin to descend slowly past Bygrave Plantation on your left. Later you pass a grass landing strip and two small hangars on your left. The track turns right and then left to continue along the lefthand side of the field down to a path post, with a stone-age axe (the Icknield Way logo) on. Turn right along the track to the Claybush Road, 1/4 mile away.

Turn left along the road, formerly known as the Bygrave Road. Gently ascend and pass The Knoll house on your right. Less than 1/4 mile later pass a stone barn on your left and immediately after turn left onto a track - still on the Icknield Way - "Partridge Hill 3/4 mile". In a short distance turn right at a small building and ascend the grass track with a hedge on your right, as you gently climb the edge of Claybush Hill. On the summit plateau you have extensive views left (westwards) and ahead to Arbury Banks. The bank edges of the fort are outlined by a hedge/fence. Keep ahead descending and soon keep to the righthand path by the field edge. Pass the path on your left to Arbury Banks - it goes past only. The path now becomes a hedged one and then a track to the bungalow at Partridge Hall. Turn right onto a hedged track with houses on your left. Later the path keeps to the right of a No Through Road - Ashwell Street, houses 58-108. At the end gain Bear Lane, here you leave the Icknield Way and turn left down the lane, past Ashwell Primary School, and where the road turns left, keep ahead, still on Bear Lane to Ashwell High Street and your first historic building, Bear House - 15th. century with some timber carvings behind a screen, on your left.

Turn right along High Street. Pass the Rose & Crown Inn and just before a 15th. century row of overhanging buildings, with a bakery, turn left onto a path by house no. 60 - Two Brewers. (Just ahead along the High Street is the Guild House, with plaster work dated 1681). In a short distance reach Swan Street and the Ashwell Village Museum on your left - an exceptionally fine timbered building. Further left is the Ashwell Cottage gardens, bought in 1968. Turn right along Swan Street and where it turns right, keep left now in Hodwell. Immediately on your left is a path to the church - St. Mary's, but before taking it, continue along Hodwell street. Pass The Rectory on the left and then Pleasant Place on the corner, with the village Lockup, opposite. On its right is a path to Ashwell Springs; follow the path to them and on the way pass the garden of the Three Tuns Inn on the right. Retrace your steps back to Hodwell and on past The Rectory to the church path, now on your right. Turn right to the church.

After your visit turn left along the path to the lynch gate. Turn right and immediately pass the Bushel and Strike Inn. Immediately turn left - "Gardiners Lane 50 yards", and walk through the car park to the lane. Turn right and pass Merchant Taylor's Close with a memorial seat on the right. Continue along the lane to Chain Cottage on the corner of Rollys Lane on your right. Bear left and on your right can be seen the splendid Ashwell Bury and grounds. At the next corner keep left and pass The Grange on your right. In 1/4 mile where the lane turns right, turn left onto a signed path. Keep the fence on your left to a stile. Soon after bear right across a stream and continue on a grass path which soon turns left then right to a footbridge and hedged path. Turn left along the path - Byway No. 7 - to reach Hinxworth Road with Holme Park Stud on your right. Turn left and walk along the road to just before the road junction and just before the house West Point. Turn right, as bridlepath signed.

Gently ascend the grass track by the hedge on your left, as you ascend Newnham Hill. Behind you, you have views back to Ashwell village. Keep by the hedge for a mile close to the summit at spot height 84m. Here views northwards unfold. Follow the grass track by the hedge as it bends left and slowly descends to a track and bridlepath post. You have views to stone tower of Hinxworth church. Turn right and keep the hedge on your left and follow the track for a mile; it weaves right and left to reach woodland and grounds of Hinxworth Place on your left. At the historic house and drive, turn left past it to where the road turns right.

Here keep straight ahead, as path signed. Follow a faint path across the field to a hedge and continue with it on your right to its end. Here is another path post. Turn left across the field, but no path line. Aim for the far electric pole and cross a dyke. Here there is a more defined path which keeps to the right of woodland around Meadow Cottage. Here the path bears right, again aiming towards the church tower of Caldecote church and Manor House beyond. Keep right along the edge of the field, passing the church a remains of a water filled moat on your left. Soon after bear right on another path that aims for the righthand of an electric pylon. Cross a footbridge and keep right to a hedge and then left to walk along beside the hedge, along the lefthand side of the field to a gate and A1 road.

The road is a dual carriageway here, with the central crash barrier split - twice , to allow you to walk through. Be patient and take great care and wait until there is a good gap in the traffic before crossing the first carriageways - traffic coming from your right. Cross through the barrier and wait again until safe to cross the other carriageways - traffic coming from the left. Stride over the barrier by the path sign and descend steps - you are now in Bedfordshire. keep straight ahead with the hedge on your right. Cross a track and pass a post path sign as the path becomes a hedge/fence path. Finally it curves left to Wrayfields road, opposite a house dated 1902. To your left is Wrayfields House, which was Brick kiln Cottage dated 1849.

Turn right along the road and in a short distance turn right long Malt House Lane towards Stotfold. Cross Ford Bridge over the River Ivel, with a car park on the right. Turn left, as path signed - Mill Lane 3/4 mile - and now walk near the river on your left, as you follow the Kingfisher Way. The path is well signed as you walk near the river at first, then leave it to walk past woodland on your left and a school to your right. Soon after keep left on the path to reach a kissing gate and Mill Lane. The mill on the left dates from 1750 and had a waterwheel 16 ft. wide, believed to be the widest in England.

Turn left then right by the Coach House to a kissing gate and continue on the path with the river well to your left and houses on your right. Follow it to a Weak Bridge. Turn left across it along a former road and before the A507 road, turn right - path signed Radwell 1/2 mile. Follow the path to steps and the road. Cross with care and descend steps to continue on the Kingfisher Way. The river is to your right, hidden by woodland. The path is well marked with yellow topped posts. Cross a drive and avenue of trees with the Mill House to your right, as you step back into Hertfordshire.

Continue by a lake, hidden by trees on your right to a kissing gate. Continue along the edge of the field to another kissing gate and road. Turn left and pass Radwell's, All Saints church (c1218), which is well worth a visit. Just after turn right, along the drive, as footpath signed and walk through Radwell Bury Farm. At the end of the buildings, turn right towards the righthand corner of the field. Here turn left and in 100 yards, right at the path post, and descend steps and follow the path to a bridge over the River Ivel. Over the first bridge turn left through a kissing gate and follow the path back to Radwell Meadows Car Park.

ICKNIELD WAY - The "Oldest road in Britain", dating from Prehistoric times. The way, some 100 miles, runs from Ivanhoe Beacon (the end of the Ridgeway) to the Peddar's Way, near Thetford, Norfolk.

ARBURY BANKS - Iron Age fort, basically 300 yards by 200 yards. The V shaped ditch has been excavated and measured 16 ft. deep by 20 ft. wide. From aerial photographs hut circles inside the fort have been seen.

The Guildhall, Ashwell. The plasterwork front dates from 1681.

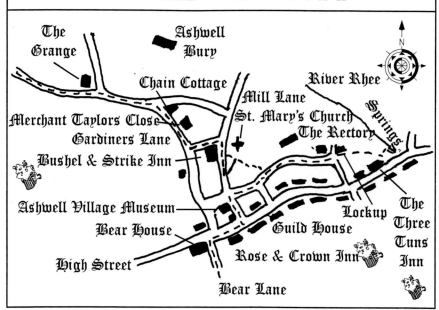

ASHWELL VILLAGE MAP

The Grange
Ashwell Bury
Chain Cottage
Mill Lane
River Rhee
St. Mary's Church
Merchant Taylors Close
Gardiners Lane
The Rectory
Springs
Bushel & Strike Inn
Ashwell Village Museum
Bear House
Lockup
Guild House
The Three Tuns Inn
High Street
Rose & Crown Inn
Bear Lane

ASHWELL -

Bear House - 15th. century with fine timber carvings behind a screen.

Rose & Crown Inn - late medieval - dates from the 16th. century.

Foresters Cottage - medieval was restored in 1962/3.

Guild House - dates from the late 15th. century and used by the St. John the Baptist Guild. The plaster work on the front is dated 1681.

The Museum -was formerly the Town House, is a two bay gabled 16th. century timbered building.

The lock up - dates from 1800 and made from chancel stones from the church - Totternoe chalk. The plaque tells the story of a local Amos Paramentor, who stayed for a few hours in the lockup. It is one of only four left to Hertfordshire.

Ashwell Springs - the source of the River Rhee/Cam. The name Ashwell, means a spring or well by ash trees.

St. Mary's church - is renowned for its graffiti from the Plague years and for a sketch of St. Paul's Cathedral, before it was burnt down in the Great Fire of London in 1666, on the north wall of the tower. There is also further graffiti to be seen on the pillars. The interior is large and airy with little stained glass and the pulpit dates from 1627. The high tower - 176 feet - has an octagonal lantern and is topped by the traditional Hertfordshire spike, and can be seen from a considerable distance away.

Merchant Taylor's Close; the main house was a school founded by the Merchant Taylor's Co., London. The school closed in 1947 and used as a Study Centre until 1968. The company sold the house in 2002 and is now a private house.

Ashwell Bury - Victorian mansion remodelled by Lutyens between 1922-6.

The Ashwell Village Museum.

St. Mary,s Church tower - Ashwell.

The Lock-up - Ashwell.

HINXWORTH PLACE - Dates from the late 15th. century and is one the finest chalk Manor Houses in Hertfordshire. The building has monastic architecture and was once used by monks. The rear of the building has "cloisters" type arches.

CALDECOTE MANOR AND CHURCH - The site of a deserted village and at the time of Domesday Book was known as Caldecota, and was once a Roman settlement. Following excavations the village appears to have been largely abandoned in the early 15th. century. The church dedicated to St. Mary Magdalene, dates from the late 14th. century.

THE KINGFISHER WAY - 32 km./20 miles from the River Ivel source at Ivel Springs, Baldock to Roxton Lock where it joins the River Great Ouse in Bedfordshire.

ALL SAINTS CHURCH, RADWELL - Dates back to the early 13th. century, when the first Rector was Baldricus in 1218. The present buildings dates from about 1340, with the Chancel arch. The small church measures just 55 feet long, with the Chancel being 13 ft. 6 inches wide and the Nave 16 ft. 6 inches. Thankfully the church overlooked through turbulent times and its magnificent memorials remain untouched. Of particular note is the Parker Memorial, 1595; Sir William Plomer, 1625; and Mary Plomer, 1605. The latter gave birth to six sons and four daughters, but here eleventh birth ended her short life at the age of 30.

Mary Plomer, 1605, memorial in Radwell church. She gave birth to six sons and four daughters - see the bottom of the memorial. Her eleventh birth ended her short life at the age of 30.

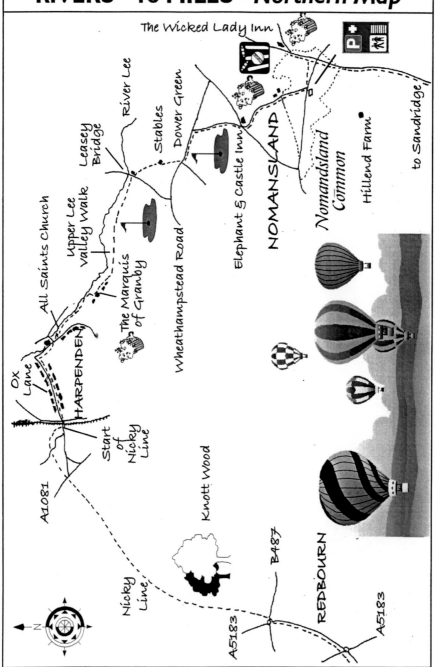

The Wicked Lady Inn

NOMANSLAND

Nomansland Common

Hillend Farm

to Sandridge

River Lee

Leasey Bridge

Stables

Dower Green

Upper Lee valley walk

All Saints Church

The Marquis of Granby

Elephant & Castle Inn

Wheathampstead Road

Ox Lane

HARPENDEN

Start of Nicky Line

A1081

Knott Wood

Nicky Line

B487

REDBOURN

A5183

A5183

N

NOMANSLAND
- OLD RAILWAYS
AND RIVERS
- 18 MILES
- allow 7 hours.

Basic route - Nomansland Common - Nomansland - Amwell - Down Green - Leasey Bridge - Upper Lea Valley Walk - Harpenden - Nicky Line - Redbourn - Ver-Colne Valley Walk - Redbournbury Mill - Shafford Mill - A5183 - Gorhambury Walk - Roman Theatre - St. Albans - Batch Wood - A1081 - Harpenden Road - Cheapside Farm - Sandridgebury - Sandridge - Nomansland Common.

Map - O.S. 1:25,000 Explorer Series No. 182 - St. Albans & Hatfield.

Car park and start - Nomansland Common, opposite the junction of Down Green Lane and Ferrers Lane. Grid Ref. 182/172124.

Inns - The Elephant and Castle, Amwell. The Marquis of Granby, Harpenden. The Green Man, The Rose & Crown Inn and The Queens Head, Sandridge. The Wicked Lady, Nomansland.

Cream Teas - seasonal; Redbournbury Mill.

ABOUT THE WALK - Sometimes you hit the jackpot! For some strange reason I was reluctant to do this walk, thinking there was not much to see. How wrong I was; this was one walk I didn't want to end. The whole walk went like clockwork and was most attractive countryside. The weather was perfect, a blue cloudless day around 24°C, with bluebells in profusion. Although late April the cricket teams were out, and as one player remarked, while playing a friendly between Wheathampstead and Sandridge, *"Normally we* *would be wearing two pullovers instead of just a shirt."* Whilst the walk follows old railways and rivers this is only part of the story. You start from a marvellous area of open land - Nomansland Common - the haunt of highwaymen and women. You follow a section of the Upper Lee Valley Walk before walking almost half of the Nicky Line to Redbourn. Here you join the Ver-Colne Valley Walk, which takes you past two stunning water mills, while walking along one of the finest river valleys in Hertfordshire, You skirt the western side of St. Albans, passing the Roman Theatre and views to the cathedral. The final part, over the fields brings you to the attractive village of Sandridge, with three inns. The final mile returns you to Nomansland Common with perhaps a visit to the historic Wicked Lady Inn?

WALKING INSTRUCTIONS - Starting from the Nomansland Common car park, return to the entrance and cross to your right to Down Green Lane. Follow the lane across the wooded area of the common, past the houses of Nomansland on the right, in 1/4 mile. Keep ahead to the hamlet of Amwell and cross roads, with the Elephant and Castle Inn on the right. Go straight across, as signed - Down Green 1/2 mile. You soon pass the pay and play, Wheathampstead Golf Course on your left. Reaching the road junction and Harpenden Road, turn left. Walk with care for this is a busy road despite being a minor road. Pass the golf course entrance on the left and shortly afterwards reach a road triangle and Pipers Lane on the left. Turn right and follow the path diagonally left across the field to a farm track and stables on the right. Here you join the Upper Lee Valley Walk. Turn right and left to a kissing gate and continue on a defined path to another kissing gate. Continue ahead, now descending to another kissing gate, house and road. Turn left down the house drive to the road and right to Leasey Bridge.

Don't cross but turn left onto the former Harpenden - Wheathampstead railway line, now part of the Upper Lee Valley Walk; the River Lee is to your right. Path signed - Batford Mill 1 mile; Harpenden 1 1/2 miles. Pass another golf course on your left and in 3/4 mile (15 mins), cross a road bridge with sewage works on the left. A short distance later turn right, as signed, and descend steps and curve left to Marquis Lane. Follow the lane left to the Marquis of Granby Inn. Turn right and left before the river bridge, and follow the Lee path with the river on the right. Pass a play area on the left and continue to a kissing gate and All Saints church, walking through the car park to the road - Station Road. Here is a plaque to the restored path and tree planting, erected in 1971. - The Upper Lea Valley Group.

Turn right and where the main road turns right, keep straight ahead into Cold

Harbour Lane, with the building, Waterside, on the right. In a few yards turn left, as path signed, and right almost immediately to regain the former railway line. At first it is a path then tarmaced. In 1/4 mile come to your first road bridge and at its far end turn left and descend steps to the lane - Ox Lane. Turn right and follow the lane uphill past houses, for 1/2 mile to a road junction and railway line. Cross to your left and walk over the road bridge over the railway line to the other side and the start the Nicky Line. Turn right and descend steps down to the former line that linked Harpenden with Hemel Hempstead. You now follow the line for the next three miles to Redbourn. First you are in a wooded cutting but after a mile you leave the outskirts of Harpenden and walk in delightful countryside, which is also part of the Chiltern Way. Pass Knott Wood on your left and more than 1/4 mile later reach the B487 road and roundabout junction with the A5183.

Cross aiming for the righthand side of the lefthand road - A5183. Here you rejoin The Nicky Line, with the road on your left. In more than 1/2 mile cross a bridge with the centre of Redbourn to your right. 200 yards later as you approach a factory on the right, turn left as path signed - Ver Valley Walk. Gain the B487 road and cross to a path sign and Chequer Lane. Here you join the Hertfordshire Way.

Follow the lane a few yards and where it turns left keep ahead on the track which becomes a path with a hedge on your left. You now follow the Ver-Colne Valley Walk all the way to edge of St. Albans, some four miles away. The path/track curves left to Mill House and Mill Stream Barn before the A5183, St. Albans Road. Go straight across to a kissing gate - Redbournbury Mill 1/2 mile. The path keeps beside the hedge on the left and later curves right to a kissing gate and Redbournbury Mill - seasonal cream teas; bakery and open to the public.

Walk past the mill and turn left and keep left to a footbridge over a stream and onto another; to your right is Redbournbury, part of the Crown Estate. After the second footbridge bear right - path signed St. Albans 2 1/2 miles. In a few yards the lane turns left, keep straight ahead on the Ver path. Reach a kissing gate and continue ahead with the hedge/fence on your left. Pass an environment site on your left and reach another kissing gate, now with the River Ver on your right. The river is you companion for the next 1 1/2 miles; popular with grey herons and kingfishers - both of whom I saw. In less than 1/

NOMANSLAND - OLD RAILWAYS AND RIVERS - 18 MILES - *Southern Map*

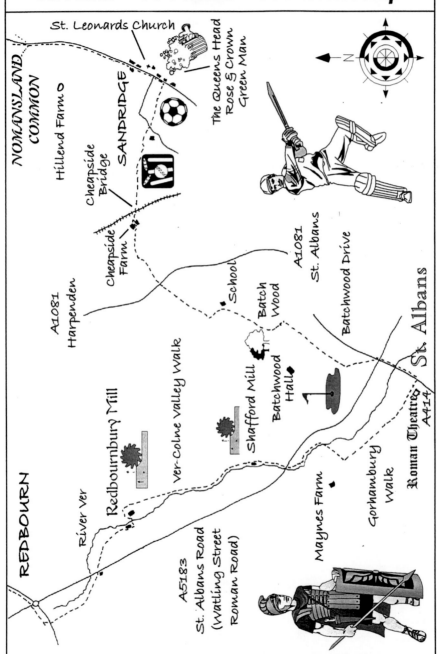

St. Leonards Church

NOMANSLAND COMMON

Hillend Farm

SANDRIDGE

Cheapside Bridge

Cheapside Farm

The Queens Head
Rose & Crown
Green Man

N

A1081 Harpenden

School

Batch Wood

A1081 St. Albans

Batchwood Drive

Redbournbury Mill

Ver-Colne Valley Walk

Shafford Mill

Batchwood Hall

St. Albans

REDBOURN

River Ver

A5183 St. Albans Road (Watling Street Roman Road)

Maynes Farm

Gorhambury Walk

Roman Theatre
A414

2 mile the path joins a lane and continue ahead passing Shafford Farm and outstanding mill building. Continue past it to the A5183 road.

Go straight across, with Bow Bridge to your right. Continue on the Ver path which takes you through woodland and near the river on the right. In 1/2 mile reach a water gauge station and junction of the Gorhambury Walk. Turn right over a bridge and now on a tarmaced drive, follow it to a T junction with Maynes Farm to the right. Turn left, as path signed, and walk along the tree lined drive for less than a mile to the Roman Theatre; as you walk, you have fine views to St. Albans Cathedral. Pass the theatre and reach the road at St. Michael's. If you go straight across you come to the Roman Museum.

Turn left along the A4147 road - Bluehouse Hill. Cross the River Ver and reach a roundabout. Opposite on the left is the St. Albans city sign and an old milepost - London 21 miles; Redbourn 3 miles. Go straight across to Batchwood Drive and in a few yards left, as bridlepath signed and part of the Hertfordshire Way; the drive leads to Batchwood Hall.

In 1/4 mile the drive reaches the top of the slope, here on the right is a bridlepath sign. Turn right and now walk beside trees on the right along the edge of the golf course. basically keep straight ahead; there are marker posts, and pass between two fairways, aiming for a group of horse chestnut trees. After, pass a path post and cross a drive and ascend to a gate gap on the edge of course. Go through and turn left, keeping a hedge on your left and the houses of New Greens to your right.

Reaching Batch Wood, following the path right. Keep to the righthand side of the wood, following paths. The wood was carpeted with bluebells in late April and is an ancient semi-natural wood. Beyond the wood keep to the edge of a football field, before passing the changing rooms on the left - path signed Bridleway 1 - Harpenden 3 miles. Soon pass another football pitch on the left, with the school on the right. Follow the path by the hedge left to another bridlepath sign. Follow it right, now a wide fenced path. Pass woodland on your left and reach a gate. Continue ahead on the defined path/track and walk through a fruit farm, past raspberry, strawberry, gooseberry and currant plants to the Harpenden Road - A1081.

41

Go straight across, as bridlepath signed, and walk along the drive to Cheapside Farm. Pass cricket fields on your right and follow the drive left then right to Cheapside Farm. As signed on the building, turn left and soon right on a track to cross the railway line via Cheapside Bridge. Keep ahead on the track with extensive views as you descend gently to Sandridgebury. Reaching the lane here, go straight across and cross the lefthand side of the field to a stile and onto another in the lefthand corner. Continue ahead and pass the football field and cricket area before gaining the road in Sandridge, near the Green Man Inn. Turn left and pass The Rose and Crown Inn and shortly afterwards on the right is St. Leonard's Church and The Queens Head Inn.

Continue on the road out of the village passing Jessamine Cottages and Tara Retreat on the left. Soon after on the left is footpath no. 3 - Nomansland Common 3/4 mile. The path keeps beside the hedge and road on the right. In 3/4 mile approach Nomansland Common and steps. Just after keep to the righthand path along the righthand side of the common; to your left can be seen the car park. You can either return there or keep ahead and cross Ferrers Lane and visit the Wicked Lady Inn close to the cricket field. Retrace your steps, turning right back to car park.

THE WICKED LADY, NOMANSLAND - Perhaps the most famous Highway women - Katherine, Lady Ferrers - who has been immortalised in two films, one starring Margaret Lockwood and James Mason. Lady Ferrers lived alone, following a failed marriage at Markyate Cell, some 8 miles west of here. According to the story she met a farmer, Ralph Chaplin, who was a highwayman at night. He taught her the crafts of his trade and she went about her secret business. One night she stopped a waggon near Nomansland but was shot in the hold-up. She limped away and died at Markyate Cell. Ralph Chaplin was also shot on one of his raids in North London at Finchley Common. The inn sign reminds us of her last outing and it is said that her ghost has been seen galloping around Nomansland.

NOMANSLAND COMMON - Named after the land here between the Abbots of St. Albans and Abbotts of Westminster - being No Man's Land.

THE NICKY LINE - Former railway line linking Harpenden, Redbourn and Hemel Hempstead.

REDBOURNBURY WATERMILL - A mill has been here since Domesday times. Until the middle of the 20th. century it was operating with Ivy Hawkins being known as, *"The last lady miller in England."* The present building dates from the 18th. century and is the last working mill on the River Ver. The mill was sold in 1986 and was badly damaged by fire the following year. Now fully restored the mill is once again grinding flour with its own Bakery. The mill is open on Sunday afternoons from mid April to early October. 2. p.m. to 5.30 p.m. and on bank holiday weekends, usually 10.30 a.m. to 5.30 p.m.

River Ver and Shafford Mill.

ROMAN THEATRE OF VERULAMIUM - One of only two in Britain. Now fully excavated and partly reconstructed you can see how it was once, with stage and dressing rooms. Nearby is the site of the Roman town of Verulamium; finds and the Roman story can be seen in the Museum at St. Michael's.

SANDRIDGE - The church dedicated to St. Leonard is of Saxon origin and contains Roman bricks. The chancel was rebuilt in the 14th. century and the Chancel Screen is particularly attractive. The tower collapsed in 1688 and rebuilt in the 19th. century.

WHITWELL, KNEBWORTH, PRESTON, KING'S WALDEN AND ST. PAUL'S WALDEN - 18 MILES

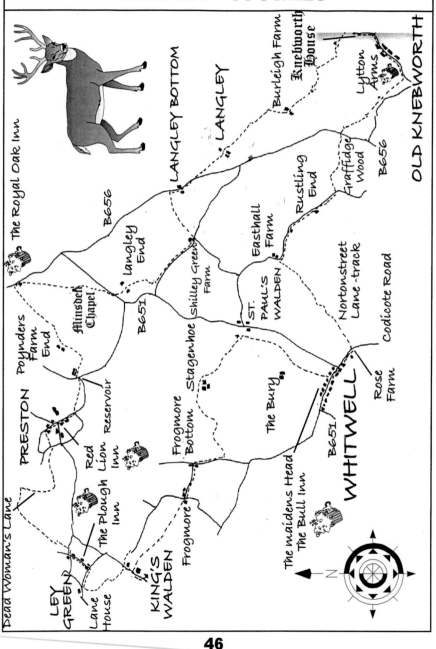

WHITWELL, KNEBWORTH, PRESTON, KING'S WALDEN AND ST. PAUL'S WALDEN
- 18 MILES
- allow 7 hours.

Basic route - Whitwell - Nortonstreet Lane - Easthall Farm - Rusling End - Graffidge Wood - B656 - Knebworth Deer Park - Old Knebworth - Knebworth House and Church - Wintergreen Wood - Burleigh Farm - Langley - Langley Bottom - B656 - Shilley Green Farm - Langley End - Minsden Chapel and Plantation - B656 - The Royal Oak Inn, Chapelfoot - Poynders End - Preston - Dead Woman's Lane - Cox Green - The Plough Inn - Ley Green - King's Walden - Kingswalden Park - Frogmore - Frogmore Bottom - Park Wood - St. Paul's Walden (Church) - Hertfordshire Way - Whitwell.

Map - O.S. 1:25,000 Explorer Series No. 193 - Luton & Stevenage.

Car park and start - Whitwell main street, near inns; roadside parking only.

Inns - The Maidens Head, The Bull Inn; Whitwell. The Lytton Arms, Old Knebworth. The Royal Oak Inn, Chapelfoot (B656). The Red Lion Inn, Preston. The Plough Inn, Ley Green. One final one in St. Paul's Walden, off the route.

ABOUT THE WALK - A remarkable unspoilt area of gentle rolling landscape, liberally sprinkled with fascinating churches and historic buildings. A mixture of paths and tracks, on "ridges" and through woodland, with red deer to be seen in Knebworth Park. The walk too has several inns including the Royal Oak Inn at Chapelfoot, approximately half way. You pass many impressive mansions, including Knebworth House, whose church has the finest sculptures in Hertfordshire, of the Lytton family. St, Paul's Walden is the area the late Queen Mother was brought up and often walked these paths; the churchyard

47

has a memorial to her. It is a walk to savour along good paths with much to see on the way. The route starts on the main street of Whitwell and is done in anticlockwise direction.

WALKING INSTRUCTIONS - Walk southwards along the main street, out of the village, along the road to Codicote. Pass Mill House on the your left and the Hertfordshire Way sign - this is your return path. Pass the road to St. Paul's Walden (B651) and War Memorial on your left. Continue on the Codicote Road out of the village to the timber framed Rose Farm. Turn left, at the Public Byway sign (BOAT), and ascend the track of Nortonstreet Lane. Pass a Sewage Works on the left, soon after leaving the road. Ascend gently and soon after levelling off walk through woodland, keeping ahead on the track as it turns left then right. Leaving the trees, continue ahead on the track and little over 1/2 mile later reach a minor road with Easthall Farm opposite. Turn right along the single track lane, and take the fourth signed right of way on your left. First pass a house on your right, then Rusling End Farm and soon after Rusling End Cottage. Pass Keepers Cottage and just after, before the road turns right, turn left onto the fourth right of way, along a track into Graffidge Wood. In a short distance, as path post signed, turn right along a path and basically keep straight ahead, crossing a track and onto another. Just after you join the track and keep ahead along in past pine trees to the B565 road (London Road).

Go straight across, as path signed, and onto a tall kissing gate. Through, enter Knebworth Deer Park and no doubt see some red deer, that roam here. Keep right by the fence to another tall kissing gate. Continue ahead along the righthand side of the field with views to your left of Knebworth House and church. Pass a Cenotaph, with a moving epitaph, on the left at the end of an avenue of trees - see sketch. Continue along the righthand side of the field - fence - to a kissing gate and onto another. Keep ahead, now with the fence on your left to the Knebworth road and Park Gate House. Turn left along the road into Old Knebworth. Pass a row of five almshouses built in 1856, and then the Lytton Arms. Pass the former entrance to Knebworth House, with the East and West Jubilee Lodges, on your left. Soon after the road forks at the Manor House; keep to the lefthand one. Follow it right later, past The Rectory and cricket field on your right. Immediately on your left is the footpath sign and kissing gate. Turn left and keep straight ahead to Knebworth Church, dedicated to St. Mary.

Walk past the church parking area and onto the churchyard - a visit is highly recommended. At the tower turn left to a gate and parkland of Knebworth

Dedicated by her grateful son
to the memory of
Elizabeth Bulwer Lytton
December 9 A.D. 1842

Source of my life, upon its morn and noon
Shedding the light that dwells in parent eyes,
Now in the shadows of its eve, I fear
Towards griefless stars this monument of thee,
Emblem of memories raised by Christian hopes
Far above craves. Mark, how serene in heaven
The upright column leaves the funeral urn.
Edward Bulwer Lytton
May 25 A.D. 1866

House. Keep ahead and join the drive towards the house, to an avenue of trees on the right, with concrete drive. Turn right down the avenue to the bottom and woodland and lake. Don't go in, turn left keeping the fence on your right. Where the fence turns right, bear right on the path and cross a small causeway to another tall deer kissing gate. Enter Wintergreen Wood, and keep right on the path. Later keep left along the path and out of the wood. Continue now on a grass track as you head towards Burleigh Farm. Reach a stile and then onto a gate before the farm. Keep ahead to a stile and path sign. Over bear right to cross the field to a stile. Turn right and then left to continue on a track to the end of the field. Turn right then left to continue on a path by the hedge on your left to a gate and Public Byway, near Langley.

Reach the village road and keep ahead along it, following it left past the former inn on your left. Just after turn right , as footpath signed - Langley Bottom, along a fenced path. At the end, the path is lost in the large field. Basically, keep straight ahead aiming for the electric pole on the left of three spaced trees. From the pole, you can see the road towards Langley Bottom. Aim towards the lefthand corner near a solitary oak tree. Opposite it is the path sign and exit to the road. Turn right and walk along the road - B656, passing the hamlet of Langley Bottom. Pass the house Vassass on your left. Soon after turn left onto a hedged track - no right of way sign, as it is another route with public access. Follow the ascending track to Langley Lane with Shilley Green Farm on the right. Keep ahead and then right along the lane and in just over 1/2 mile (12 mins.) reach the Hertfordshire Way.

Turn right, at first a hedged path as you turn right and left along it. Then it becomes a track with the hedge on your left as you soon reach Langley End. Keep straight ahead for a few yards to where the lane turns left, opposite the house Bridle Ways. Keep ahead, as bridlepath signed and descend following the grass track right to the B651 road - you are still on the Hertfordshire Way. Cross the road and continue on a track, near the road at first, before it swings left and right to Minsden Chapel Plantation. Don't go into the wood, but keep on the path along its righthand side - beech trees - as you ascend. At the wood's end on your left can be seen the ruined walls of Minsden Chapel. Continue on the path as you start to descend. Reaching a few trees turn left and right to continue on an intermittent "hedged" path, as you descend to the Royal Oak Inn at Chapelfoot and the B656. Here you leave the Hertfordshire Way and are approximately halfway!

Turn left along the B656, passing the inn, and a few yards later left onto a track, path signed - Preston 1 1/2 miles. You gently ascend towards Poynders End, and as you do so you have fine views behind you to Stevenage on the right (east), and Hitchin to your left (north). At the top follow the path/track right around the edge of the field, passing the impressive Tudor building of Poynders End Farm, on the right. Continue with the fence on your right to a stile. Then still keep ahead by the field edge - hedge on your left. Follow the field edge round to your right to pass the grassy banks of a reservoir, on your right. Just after gain a minor road. Turn left to a T junction beside Kiln Wood Lodge. Turn right onto the Preston road, and immediately right, again, to a kissing gate and path sign - Preston 1/2 mile. The path line is faint, but aim to the left of two separate barns. Keep ahead to houses and another kissing gate and road. To your right can be seen the large building of the Princess Helena College - Girls Boarding school.

Turn right past the school entrance and into Preston and pass the Red Lion Inn. Ignore the first road on your left and soon after the road forks, with the road to Hitchin to your right. Keep left along Chequers Lane for a short distance to Chequers Cottage and footpath sign on the left. Turn left along the path and soon pass a children's play area on the left with a trim trail for the Under 6's! Keep ahead on the path to a lane beside The Willows, on the left. Turn left and in a few yards right near Hollytrees, at the kissing gate and path sign. The path bears right to pass an open wooden barn on the left - to your right is Pond Farm - before turning left to a stile. Continue with the hedge on your right to a kissing gate and track - Dead Woman's Lane.

Turn right along the hedged track, which is a Public Byway (BOAT). Ignore the first track in 1/4 mile on the left and take the next one; still a red BOAT. In 5 minutes turn left along another track, and follow it for nearly 3/4 mile to Cox Green and road. Turn right and in a few yards left, with a pond and seats on your left, and walk up Plough Lane. Pass the Plough Inn on your left. At the top reach Whitehall Road, turn right into Ley Green. Pass Laurel Cottage on your right with date stone - TFA 1896 - on the front. Soon after reach another pond and seat on your left. Immediately after, as path signed, turn left. Ahead is the road to Offley and large Lane House is on the right. The path keeps close to the hedge on the left and curves left to pass a barn and here join the track on the right. Pass through woodland and at the end turn right along a path around the edge of the field. Follow it left, with the hedge on your right and reach Church Road in King's Walden.

The route now is to your left, but first it worth seeing King's Walden church dedicated to St. Mary - the prominent tower is to your right. Also on the right is the Manor Garden Nursery with a Victorian Walled Garden - you will have seen this, on the right, as you walked to the road. Return to your earlier path and walk along the road a few yards to the path sign on the right - Frogmore 3/4 mile. On the right is the hedge of Kingswarden Bury, whose impressive house you will see next, on your right. Go through two gates and continue ahead to two kissing gates. The path bears slightly right and becomes a raised path, through the wooded parkland with sheep and long horned cattle, to a gate and "drive" from Whitehall Farm on the left. Here as path arrowed, keep ahead on another track/drive, and follow this for almost 1/2 mile to Frogmore Lodge and hamlet of Frogmore.

Keep straight ahead on the road past the houses on the left and another large duck pond on the right. Follow the road to Frogmore Bottom and T junction. Turn right onto the Whitwell Road. In 1/4 mile at White Lodge, turn left, as footpath signed. Follow the grass track, at first, as it swings left becoming a track, to a path post. Continue on the track as curves right and left to another path post and junction of paths. Turn left, now on a path, as you pass Park Wood on the left. Continue ahead to the edge of next wood - Foxholes Wood - and a path post. Turn right and soon left along the boundary fence of Stagenhoe mansion (Sue Ryder Care home) and reach the drive. Follow it left - basically straight ahead - for a short distance before turning right down a track past a tennis court and lodge. Keep on the track past woodland on the right, as you ascend gently to a tarmaced lane. Continue ahead along it and in 1/4 mile reach All Saints church, St. Paul's Walden, on the left. On the right is the Hertfordshire Way, your next and final path.

The church is well worth a visit to see the late Queen Mothers memorial in the churchyard and the church's interior. Turn right along the track, as you descend the Hertfordshire Way, to a tarmaced drive. Keep ahead along it and where the drive turns right to The Bury is a kissing gate. Go through, still on the Hertfordshire Way, and turn left to keep the fence on your left to gates before descending towards Whitwell. Reach kissing gates and cross the River Mimram and onto Mill House and road in Whitwell; the end of the walk. To your right along the High Street, is the Bull Inn and Maidens Head Inn.

WHITWELL - Attractive village with some interesting houses, notably the timber framed Bull Inn.

KNEBWORTH HOUSE - Surrounded by a 260 acre park, the estate and house have belonged to Lytton family for more than 500 years. The original Tudor mansion is hidden behind different facades over the centuries, and is today mostly Victorian. Much of the work was done by Edward Bulwer-Lytton, the first Lord Lytton, who inherited the house in 1843.

The church dedicated to St. Mary and St. Thomas, is one of the most interesting in Hertfordshire. Inside are 15th. century pews and a Georgian pulpit with 16th. century Flemish panels. But the glory of the church is the Lytton Chapel. All around the walls are beautifully sculptured monuments of the 17th. and 18th. century of various Lyttons - see above. The workmanship is breathtaking.

MINSDEN CHAPEL - Recorded in the Domesday Book as Menlesdene: King's land, formerly Earl Harold. The site of a deserted village. The flint walls of the chapel rise to between 10 and 20 feet high.

PRESTON - St. Martins church was built in 1900. Inside are monuments from Temple Dinsley.

Temple Dinsley is the site of a Preceptory of the Knights Templar, founded in 1147 by Bernard de Balliol. The building was later demolished and the present building dates from 1714 and includes much work, later, by Lutyens. The Princess Helena College which now occupies the building, began in 1935, and is a girls boarding school.

KING'S WALDEN - St. Mary's church dates back to the 13th. century with a late 13th. century Chancel Arch.

King Walden Bury was a large Neo Elizabethan building built between 1889-90 and designed by Burmeister and Beeston. This was replaced by the present large Neo Georgian mansion by Raymond Firth and Quinton Terry.

Kingwalden Bury.

ST. PAUL'S WALDEN - In Walden Bury, Elizabeth Angela Marguerite Bowes-Lyon was born. She grew up here before marrying the Duke of York and later becoming Queen to George VI in 1936. Their children were Princess Elizabeth and Margaret. The former becoming the present Queen in 1953. A tall white memorial to the former Queen Mother is in All Saints churchyard - on the right of the above photo. Inside the Perpendicular church can be seen memorials to Bowes-Lyon family and the font the late Queen Mother was baptised in, in 1900. Also to be seen is a Baroque screen by an unknown artist. The mediaeval tower is capped by the traditional Hertfordshire spike.

AYOT ST. LAWRENCE AND THE RIVER LEE - 15 MILES

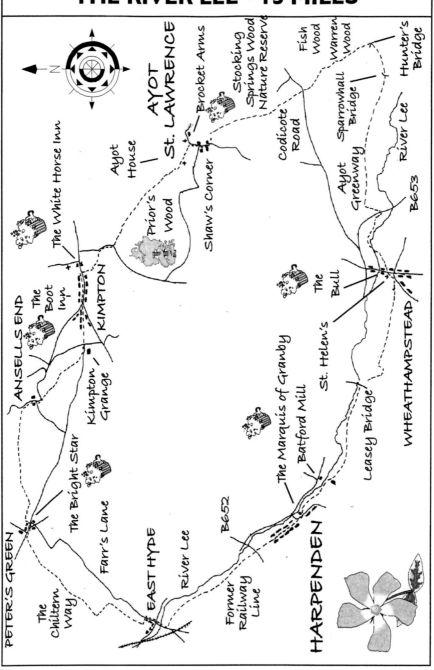

AYOT ST. LAWRENCE
AND THE RIVER LEE
- 15 MILES
- allow 6 to 7 hours.

Basic route - Ayot St. Lawrence - Stocking Springs Wood - Codicote Road - Fish Wood - Warren Wood - Hunter's Bridge - Ayot Greenway - Robinson Wood - B653 - River Lee - Wheathampstead - Leasey Bridge - Former Railway - Harpenden - River Lee Walk - East Hyde - The Chiltern Way - Peter's Green - Perry Green - Cannons Farm, Ansells End - Kimpton Grange - Kimpton - Claggbottom Wood - Prior's Wood - Ayot St. Lawrence.

Map - O.S. 1:25,000 Explorer Series No. 182 - St. Albans & Hatfield.

Car Park and start - Roadside parking in Ayot St. Lawrence - between the ruined St. Lawrence church and the Brocket Arms.

Inns - Brocket Arms, Ayot St. Lawrence. The Bull, Wheathampstead - Marquis of Granby, Harpenden. The Bright Star, Peter's Green. The Boot Inn and The White Horse Inn, Kimpton.

ABOUT THE WALK - I did this walk on the hottest April day in living memory, and apart from the many attractive buildings and rolling countryside I saw, the woods were carpeted with bluebells - a joy from start to finish. Part of the object of the walk is to walk part of the Lea Valley Walk to the Bedfordshire boundary at East Hyde. Starting from Ayot St. Lawrence you walk past delightful woodland to the Lee Valley and follow the Ayot Greenway - former railway line - to Wheathampstead. Walking through this historical village you walk above the river to Leasey Bridge and River Lee. Now back on the railway line you follow it close to the river, through Harpenden and onto East Hyde. leaving the river you ascend gently following a segment of the Chiltern Way to Peter's Green, with Luton Airport just over the trees. Now heading eastwards you pass the attractive hamlet of Ansells End - a collection of farms - before descending to the attractive historical village of Kimpton. Now on your final section you descend to pine woodland and ascend gently back to your start; the absorbing village of Ayot St. Lawrence, with ruined church, an impressive Greek Revival style church and George Bernard Shaw's house - National Trust property. The whole route follows well defined paths with views and passes numerous inns!

WALKING INSTRUCTIONS - Starting from the road beside the ruined St. Lawrence's church in Ayton St. Lawrence, walk past the church to the Ruins Cottage on the corner - this is your return point. Follow the road left and pass Shaw's House on your right. Keep ahead, descending to where the road turns left beside Amesbury House. Just round the corner turn left onto a well defined bridlepath - Codicote Road 3/4 mile and Ayot Greenway 2 miles - both your destinations. The bridleway soon becomes a hedged path as it curves right and is a path/track most of the time. After nearly 3/4 mile you pass Stocking Spring Wood - Nature reserve of the Hertfordshire & Middlesex Wildlife Trust - a traditional coppiced hornbeam woodland. You can walk through the wood paralleling the bridleway. At the end both paths meet at Codicote Road.

Go straight across and continue on the bridleway - Hunter's Bridge 3/4 mile. The wide path keeps woodland on your left; first Dowdell's Wood, then Fish Wood and Warren Wood. The later you walk through with Bladder Wood on the right. Leaving the woodland behind you approach Hunter's Bridge and the Ayot Greenway. Before the bridge turn right and ascend to the Greenway and keep right along it. You keep on it for the next 1 1/2 miles. In 1/4 mile pass under Sparrowhall Bridge and in another 1/4 mile pass Robinson's Wood with picnic tables on the left. Continue ahead on the Greenway and a mile later (20 mins) reach a cross roads on tracks. Turn left, as signed Cycle route and walk through the tunnel of the B653 road. Keep ahead a little further before turning right along a fenced path, and now on the Lee Valley walk. Continue to a gate and turn left along the defined path by a fence to near the River Lee, on your left. Just after the path forks and keep left to walk close to the river to a footbridge. Cross over and bear right onto a track which becomes a tarmaced lane - Meads Lane - and follow it to the main road in Wheathampstead, with The Bull Inn on the right.

Turn left and in a short distance, right to walk through the churchyard and pass St. Helen's church on the right, to reach the top of the churchyard. Turn right and pass the Old School, Bury Green. In 100 yards turn left into High Meads and right almost immediately - Leasey Bridge 1 mile. All the time guided by the Lee Valley Walk signs - Swans. The defined path leads away from Wheathampstead to kissing gates with views to your right. The path turns left then right to stables on the left. Turn right here to a kissing gate and descend to another and onto the road at Leasey Bridge. In the final part you walk down a house drive and turn right. Almost immediately turn left - Batford Mill 1 mile - and now back on a former railway line. Follow it for 3/4 mile with the River Lee to your right, to the start of a Sewage Works on your left. Turn right and descend steps and follow the path left to Marquis Lane. Keep ahead along this to the Marquis of Granby Inn. Turn right - ahead is Batford Mill - and turn left almost immediately to walk close to the river. Pass a children's play area on the left and later pass All Saints church on the right, now in Harpenden. Gain the road on the left - Station Road - and turn right. The road turns right almost immediately; keep straight ahead into Cold Harbour Lane and the Waterside offices on the right.

In a few yards keep left to rejoin the former railway line, which is tarmaced at first. Follow it for 1/2 mile to Bower Heath Lane and go straight across. The railway line is now a track which becomes a path later. Basically for the next 1 1/4 miles you follow the track/path - still the Lee Valley Way - with views of the river on your right. Reaching the next road Thrales End Lane, turn right to East Hyde and now briefly in Bedfordshire. Cross the road bridge over the River Lee to the road junction at Lea Bridge Corner. To your left is East Hyde church. Turn right and left and walk up Farr's Lane to the last house on your left. Turn left and join a section of The Chiltern Way. The path keeps to lefthand side of the field before turning right and ascending to a path post and crest of the Lee Valley. Turn left following a defined path with views ahead of the valley and to Luton Hoo. In 1/4 mile reach a path crossroads and turn right and follow the defined path to kissing gates and onto the village of Peter's Green, 1 1/4 miles away. To your left you can see the planes taking off and landing at Luton Airport. After a mile cross the track from a cluster of houses near Laburnum Farm, on your left. Keep ahead on the path to reach the road in Peter's Green, with the Village hall (1929) on your left; and now back in Hertfordshire.

Turn right and walk through the village towards The Bright Star Inn. But before it at Old Red Cottage on your left, turn left as path signed; still on the Chiltern Way. Pass between the houses and reaching the open field turn right along its edge past the houses to a bridlepath post. Turn left keeping the hedge on your right as you descend and curve right. The defined path later has a hedge on your left to a gate before it is on your right. Continue to a gate and road. Turn right into Ansells End, passing Cannons Farm on your left. Keep ahead to where the road turns left and here on the corner is the next path and path sign. The defined path basically keeps straight ahead for more than 1/2 mile with views leftwards to the village of Kimpton. You reach Kimpton Road opposite Kimpton Grange. Turn left to the road T junction. Go straight across onto another path and follow it straight ahead into Kimpton reaching Claggy Road with shops on your left. Turn right then left to walk along the main street. Pass The Boot Inn on the left; the War Memorial on the right; and Kimpton House on the left. Soon after at house no. 13 and before the White Horse Inn, turn right, as path signed. Ascend past a play area on the left, then a football field, and up steps to the open field; behind you you have views of Kimpton and its church.

Turn left and keep to the lefthand side of the field, first with the Bowling Green on your left. The path turns left afterwards along the field edge to above the road. Continue, now on a permissive path above the road to a path post the road. Turn left to the road corner and bear right onto track, footpath signed. Keep the hedge on your right to a post and bear right slightly to descend to Claggbottom Wood and Prior's Wood. Follow the path down and into the pine wood to a stile. Cross and ascend to the wood's edge and keep ahead with it on your right with views to Ayot House on your left. Reach a stile and turn left to a kissing gate; on your right is the present Ayot St. Lawrence church - Greek Revival design - well worth a visit. Follow the path by the fence to Ruins Cottage and turn left along the road to pass the ruined St. Lawrence church, back to your start.

Ayot St. Lawrence church.

The ruined church of Ayot St. Lawrence.

AYOT St. LAWRENCE - The old church, now a *"romantic"* folly, dates from the 12th. century and was "pulled down" by Sir Lionel Lyde of Ayton House. The new St. Lawrence church was designed by Nicholas Revett and built between 1778-9, in new Greek Revival style. In the outer aedicules stand the urns of Sir Lionel Lyde and his wife. Ayton House dates from the early 18th. century.

Shaw's Corner was formerly the New Rectory and was built during the late 19th. century. George Bernard Shaw lived here, for 44 years, and when he died in 1950, in his will he requested everything should left as it was. It is now owned by the National Trust and they have honoured his request. The Brocket Arms was once part of the Brocket estate and was, for a while, known as the Three Horseshoes. Part of the building is 15th. century and has a Kingpost roof. The inn is recorded back to 1694.

AYOT GREENWAY
- Former railway line
from Welwyn Garden
City to
Wheathampstead;
now a walking and
cycling route.

THE LEA VALLEY WALK - The river's name can be spelt either Lea or Lee. The whole walk from its source at Leagrave, near Luton to the Limehouse basin and River Thames, in eastern London, is 50 miles long. The 28 mile section from Hertford to Limehouse Basin is along the River Lee Navigation; much of this section is within the Lee Valley Regional Park.

St. Helen's church, Wheathampstead.

WHEATHAMPSTEAD - The name comes from Saxon times and means - "a house on the wet marsh." The church, dedicated to St. Helen, has Norman work and the rest dates from 1340; the spire was made in 1865. Among the many memorials is one to Apsley Cherry-Garrard, renowned for finding Capt. Scott's body in the Antarctic. The Garrard family lived nearby for some 400 years. The Bull Inn dates from 1717.

HARPENDEN - Has connections with actor's and actress's; Eric Morecambe's was a resident and the church, dedicated St. Nicholas, had his funeral here in 1984. The church has a 15th. century tower but the rest was rebuilt in 1862. Batford Mill was a flour mill in 1860 and later ground bones for fertiliser. The Marquis of Granby Inn was originally known as The Swan Inn when owned by John Goodyear of Batford Mill. In 1799 it changed its name to the present one.

Marquis of Granby Inn sign, Harpenden.

EAST HYDE - The Romanesque-style church was built in 1840 and the architect was Benjamin Ferrey. He was influenced by St. Albans Cathedral. Behind the church is the Wernher mausoleum, which is similar to St. Albans shrine in the cathedral. Hyde Mill Farm, passed on the right before the village, has been a mill since Norman times.

THE CHILTERN WAY - 215 km (129 miles) walk around The Chilterns from Ewelme in the west to Hollybush Hill near Great Offley in the east.

LUTON AIRPORT - Began in 1939 and now handles several million passengers a year.

PETER'S GREEN - The Bright Star became an inn in 1850 when George Biggs, a *" victualler and grocer"*, bought it. Originally it was two houses built about 1729.

View back to Kimpton and its church.

KIMPTON - The perpendicular church, dedicated to St. Paul and St. Peter, has considerable 13th. century work. The Boot Inn dates from 1797 and The White Horse Inn became an inn in 1837, when John Marshall, a *"brewer of Hitchin"*, bought it.

Kimpton House.

"TOWN & COUNTRY"
- STANMORE & RIVER COLNE
- 20 MILES - *Southern map*

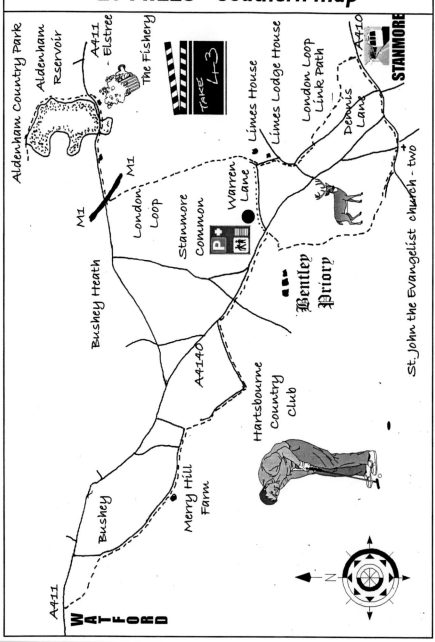

Aldenham Country Park

Aldenham Reservoir

A411 - Elstree

The Fishery

TAKE 4-3

Limes House

Limes Lodge House

London Loop Link Path

STANMORE

A410

Dennis Lane

M1

M1

London Loop

Stanmore Common

Warren Lane

Bentley Priory

St. John the Evangelist church - two

Bushey Heath

A4140

Hartsbourne Country Club

Bushey

Merry Hill Farm

A411

WATFORD

N

"TOWN & COUNTRY"
- STANMORE AND
RIVER COLNE
- 20 MILES
- allow 7 to 8 hours.

Basic route - Stanmore Underground Station - London Loop Link Path - Stanmore Country Park - Warren Lane - London Loop - MI - Aldenham Reservoir - Elstree Aerodrome - Letchmore Heath - Round Bush - Aldenham - Otterspool - River Colne - Colne Valley Linear Park - Watford - Bushey - Merry Hill - A411 - Stanmore Common - Warren Lane - London Loop - Bentley Priory - Deer Park - St. John the Evangelist Church's - A410 - Stanmore.

Map - O.S. 1:25,000 Explorer Series No. 173 - London North.

Start and end - Stanmore Underground Station - Jubilee Line. Alternative start - Warren Lane Car Park - Stanmore Common. This makes the walk about 16 1/2 miles long (allow 6 to 7 hours).

Inns - The Three Horseshoes, Letchmore Heath. The Round Bush, Round Bush - just off the route. The Victoria (Watford), A411. The Windmill, A4140 (Harvester Restaurant). The Crazy Horse Inn, Stanmore.

Cafe - Stanmore, as you return.

ABOUT THE WALK - Located in the south western corner of the county this walk explores both Town and Country walking. You start and end in Middlesex and explore part of the London Loop Recreational Path as you walk around Aldenham Reservoir. You pass the site of an Elstree Film Studio and cross the Elstree Aerodrome runway. Having left the London Loop you reach the most attractive village of Letchmore Heath, before continuing onto Round Bush, Aldenham and the River Colne. Turning south you follow the river close to the suburbia of Watford, before returning to the countryside around Merry Hill. Next you walk through an exclusive residential area to reach Stanmore Common and briefly rejoin the London Loop at Bentley Priory. Leaving it you descend through parkland past a Deer Park back to Stanmore. Here are two historical surprises, although back in Middlesex - the two St. John the Evangelist churches - the brick ruined one dates from 1632 - and Cottrell Cottages dated 1565. 1/4 mile later you are back at Stanmore Station after a very varied and interesting walk.

WALKING INSTRUCTIONS - Exiting the station go straight across the A410 road - you return along the road on your left at the end - and keep ahead in-between the hedge to Kerry Avenue and your first London Loop Link Path sign. Continue ahead passing the houses to gain the Stanmore Country Park. Bear left and keep to the lefthand side of the park, as signed. In about ten minutes reach a stile before Dennis Lane, opposite house No. 51. Turn right along the lane, as signed. At the top reach a Y junction and keep right along Wood Lane. In a short distance turn left into Warren Lane and now on the London Loop proper. Pass Limes Lodge House on the right and Limes House. Just after Warren Lane turns left - 1/4 mile along there is the car park. Keep right, as signed - Public Byway No. 6. Follow the drive to the next path sign - Elstree Road - and turn half left along the fenced path. parallel with the drive on your left. On your right are the buildings of the Royal National Orthopaedic Hospital. The path can be a little overgrown in summer, but once past the buildings, continue straight ahead now on a track, as you descend with the M1 ahead. Where the track turns right to a barn, keep ahead to the next field and ascend slightly to a London Loop path sign - you are now in Hertfordshire. Cross the field aiming for the top righthand corner, where there is a kissing gate before Elstree Road - A411.

Turn right and cross the M1 and soon pass The Waterfront Industrial Park; on the lefthand gate can be a Cinema plaque, recording this was *the site of Danzier Bros. New Elstree Studios, who made "B" movies here between 1956-61.* Continue beside the road with Aldenham Reservoir on your left. At the Fishery Inn, cross the road to the reservoir path and London Loop notice board - Section 15 - Hertmere to Harrow - see photo. Keep right along the wide path as you curve around the reservoir. Pass the sailing club and soon afterwards the London Loop turns right - you will walk a small section of the London Loop at Bentley Priory, some 10 miles away! Keep to the lefthand path beside the reservoir and across the dam wall to the car parking area of Aldenham Country Park. Keep to the righthand side of the car park and road to a stile and road. Turn right along the road and where it turns right, keep ahead along Hoggs

68

Lane. Pass Page's Farm and turn left at Footpath No. 36 and stile. The path line is faint but it is well stiled. Reach another stile and onto another with a horse riding area on the left. Keep ahead and descend to a stile and footbridge and cross the next field to a stile. Here bear half right across the field to a kissing gate beside a path sign - Hoggs Lane 400 yards.

Turn left and pass the offices of the Elstree Aerodrome on the right, with many Cessna planes and helicopters. The path is signed No. 35 - Coldharbour Lane 1 1/4 miles/Hillfield Lane 3/4 mile. Partially hidden on your left is Hillfield Park Reservoir. Follow the path for 1/4 mile to where it turns left with woodland on the left. Just after the bend reach a white sign - Beware of Aircraft. Turn right here along a small path, passing a row of three red lights, and ensuring no planes are coming or going, cross the runway to the field edge and another white sign. Keep straight ahead and soon walk through woodland as the path bears slightly left, to continue with a hedge on your right. At the end of the field cross a footbridge and basically keep straight ahead, with a line of oak trees to your left - there is a defined path on the otherside of the trees, another right of way, which joins our right of way. At the end of the field join a well defined path as you continue ahead to the far righthand corner of the field to a gap, path sign and road on the edge of Letchmore Heath.

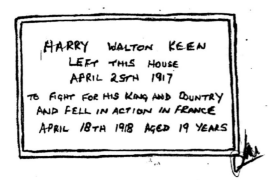

Turn left and walk through the attractive village, passing The Three Horseshoes Inn on the right and the Hare Krishna Temple compound on the left - no entry from the village. Follow the road as it curves left, passing the Old Bakery on the right - notice the poignant plaque to Harry Walton Keen; there are other plaques in the village. Pass the Aldenham War Memorial Hall on the left and soon after White Cottage. Opposite turn right at footpath No. 3 - Round Bush - and now on part of the Hertfordshire Way. Keep straight ahead along the track for 1/2 mile to Primrose Lane and the hamlet of Round Bush. Cross the road into The Spinney - Cul de Sac - and follow it to its end and gain the

"TOWN & COUNTRY"
- STANMORE & RIVER COLNE
- 20 MILES - *Northern map*

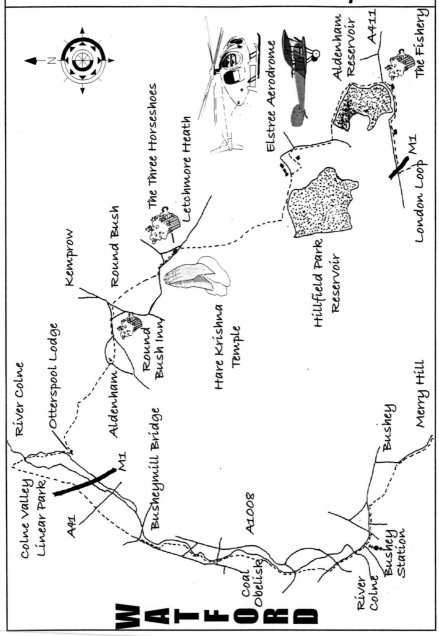

N

River Colne

Colne Valley Linear Park

Otterspool Lodge

Kemprow

Round Bush

The Three Horseshoes

Letchmore Heath

Round Bush Inn

Aldenham

M1

A41

Busheymill Bridge

Hare Krishna Temple

Coal Obelisk

A1008

Elstree Aerodrome

Hillfield Park Reservoir

Aldenham Reservoir

A411

The Fishery

London Loop M1

Bushey

Merry Hill

River Colne

Bushey Station

WATFORD

main road (B462). Continue left along it on its righthand side; the road on your left leads to the Round Bush Inn. At the next road on your right - Church Lane - cross at the junction and continue on a path which leads to Aldenham church, dedicated to St. John the Baptist, and road.

At the road here turn right and in a few yards left onto the Public Bridleway No. 77 - Brickett Wood 2 3/4 miles. At first this is the drive to the University on your right. Where it turns right keep ahead on a track which gently curves right. Follow it for 1/4 mile (5 mins) to a footpath post on the left. Turn left in woodland and follow the path through trees, with a golf course on your right. In little over 1/4 mile reach a drive and turn left along it to Otterspool Lodge. Immediately after, turn right onto another tarmaced drive with the River Colne on your left. in 200 yards turn left over a footbridge and continue now on a path with the river on your right. In 1/4 mile cross a footbridge - the righthand one - and leave the river and bear right around woodland to a kissing gate and onto a tarmaced drive; you are now on the Ver-Colne Valley Walk.

Turn left and follow the drive with views left to where your recently walked. In 1/2 mile walk over the M1. Continue to a kissing gate and the A41. Cross and continue on the tarmaced path - Footpath signed - Lower High Street 2 miles (your destination) - and part of the Colne Valley Linear Park. 1/2 mile later cross the road with Busheymill Bridge to your left; on the right are houses of Watford. Keep ahead now along a road with the River Colne on your left. Where it turns left, turn left to walk close to it around a rugby field, Pass under the next road with an Industrial Park on the right, with Sanyo offices. Continue on the tarmaced path near the river and cross another road and later pass under a railway viaduct. Just after on your right is an obelisk, marking the boundary to pay taxes for bringing coal into London. Continue by the river to the A411 and onto another road, with Tesco Extra. Keep ahead on the right of it, following the cycle signs for Rickmansworth. This path later curves right to Lower High Street.

Turn left - to your right is the central shopping area of Watford - along the road to the main road junction and traffic lights. Go straight across and where the road forks, keep left to pass Wickes and a Turnpike marker on the left. Just after walk under the railway line with Bushey Station on the right. Keep left and ascend Chalk Hill and pass The Victoria Inn on the right. Keep ahead to a Methodist church on the right. Just after turn right along Haydon Road. Where it turns right keep ahead to a gate and and triple paths by Footpath Sign No. 62 - Merryhill Road - your destination. Keep to the middle path with a hedge on the left to a footbridge. Cross and turn right to reach the Merry

71

Hill Road. Cross to Haydon Dell Farm, and follow the fenced path on the left of it - Path No. 16. In 150 yards reach a path junction and turn right along the tarmaced fenced path to regain Merry Hill Lane; opposite is Haydon Mill House.

Turn left and follow the ascending lane past St. Margarets School on the left. 1/4 mile later the road turns sharp left; turn right here onto a track - Whomsoever lane and Public Bridleway No. 52 - Prowse Avenue 380 yards. Pass Hill Mead Nature Reserve on the left. Gaining the avenue turn right and follow the path past exclusive property. In 1/4 mile it turns left, opposite the entrance to Hartsbourne Country Club, and becomes Hartsbourne Avenue as you gently ascend. Pass a magnificent fronted Tudor house dated 1517 on the left; then Hartsbourne Primary School on the right. At the top of the road gain the A4140. Turn right and soon pass The Windmill (Harvester restaurant) on your right. Just after at the junction with the A409, leave Hertfordshire and step back into Middlesex. Keep straight ahead along the righthand side of the road and soon pass Stanmore Common on your left. On your right is the entrance to Bentley Priory (RAF). A little further on your left is Warren Road with Stanmore Common Car Park partway along it.

Turn right here into Priory Drive and back, briefly, onto the London Loop. Follow the drive past exclusive property, following it right and then turning left at the footpath - Old Lodge Way - and still on the London Loop. Descend the track and in five minutes the London Loop turns right beneath Bentley Priory. Keep straight ahead and now on a tarmaced path as you descend through woodland and pass a Deer park on the left, where Roe and Munjac deer can be seen. Continue to a gate and on along the tarmaced path to a kissing gate. Keep ahead as it curves left to reach a kissing gate and Old Lodge Way. Follow the road to the A410 road and turn left. Just before the next road junction, on your right are the two St. John the Evangelist churches; the ruined brick one (1632) is beyond the present church. Keep beside the A410 past the shops of Stanmore and The Crazy Horse Inn on the left. Ignore all turnings and keep on the A410 all the way - London Road. Pass the Cottrell Cottages, dated 1565, on the right. Keep straight ahead and pass Dennis Lane on your left and soon after reach Stanmore Station.

LONDON LOOP - 150 mile walk around the country edge of the metropolis of London. The walk is split into 24 sections and can be done over one to two weeks, depending on your daily mileage. Each section has a similar board to the one here at Aldenham Country park.

LETCHMORE HEATH - Several of the cottages have memorials to servicemen who left but did not return.

Deer in Bentley Priory Deer Park.

73

COAL OBELISK -

"This obelisk was originally erected by the Corporation of London. Under the London Coal and Wine duties Act 1861. It marked the boundary for payment of taxes on the passage of coal into London. A duty of 1s. 1d. per ton was levied on all coal brought south of this mark until 1890.

Originally it was 40 metres south-west of its present site, on the opposite side of the river. Erected here in 1984.

THIS is the oldest remaining turnpike marker in Watford & is preserved within this development

SPARROWS HERNE TRUST

Watford Turpike marker, beside the A411, near Wickes.

BENTLEY PRIORY - As the name suggests this was the site of a 13th. century Augustine Priory. The present house was built in 1775. In the 1850's it was the home of the Dowager Queen Adelaide. Now it is RAF property, hence the fence and floodlights around its perimeter.

Delightful Tudor house dated 1517 on Hartsbourne Avenue.

CHURCH OF ST. JOHN THE EVANGELIST, GREAT STANMORE - The brick church was built in 1632 and served for 200 years. Lord Aberdeen, a former Prime Minister is buried here. The population out grew the church and a much larger closeby was built in 1850. The old one started to be knocked down but following a public outcry it was left as a ruin - *"The finest brick ruin in Middlesex."*

HEMEL HEMPSTEAD, FLAMSTEAD AND THE NICKY LINE - 20 miles - *Map One.*

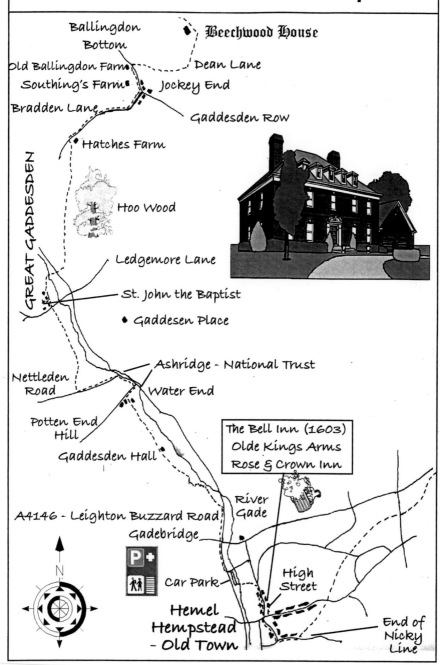

Ballingdon Bottom

Beechwood House

Old Ballingdon Farm

Dean Lane

Southing's Farm

Jockey End

Bradden Lane

Gaddesden Row

Hatches Farm

Hoo Wood

GREAT GADDESDEN

Ledgemore Lane

St. John the Baptist

Gaddesen Place

Ashridge - National Trust

Nettleden Road

Water End

Potten End Hill

Gaddesden Hall

The Bell Inn (1603)
Olde Kings Arms
Rose & Crown Inn

River Gade

A4146 - Leighton Buzzard Road

Gadebridge

Car Park

High Street

N

Hemel Hempstead - Old Town

End of Nicky Line

HEMEL HEMPSTEAD, GREAT GADDESDEN, MARKYATE, FLAMSTEAD, REDBOURN AND THE NICKY LINE - 20 MILES - all 8 hours.

Basic route - Hemel Hempstead (Leighton Buzzard Road) - Gaddesden Hall - Water End - Ashridge, National Trust Property - A4146 - Nettleden Road - Great Gaddesden - Hob Wood - Bradden Lane - Jockey End - Ballingdon Bottom - Dean Lane & Wood - Beechwood House - Kennels Lodge - Hollybush Lodge - Roe End - Markyate - Flamstead - Norringtonend Farm - M1 - Redbourn - The Nicky Line - Old Town, Hemel Hempstead - Gadebridge Park.

Map - O.S. 1:25,000 Explorer Series No. 182 - St. Albans & Hatfield.

Car Park and start - "Park & Ride", beside the Leighton Buzzard Road (A4146) next to Gadebridge Park. Grid Ref. 053083.

Inns - The Sun Inn, Markyate. The Three Blackbirds and The Spotted Dog, Flamstead. The Bell Inn, The Bull Inn, and The George in Redbourn. The Midland, Midland Road, Hemel Hempstead. The White Hart Inn, The Bell Inn (1603), Olde Kings Arms and the Rose & Crown Inn in the Old Town of Hemel Hempstead.

ABOUT THE WALK - The longest in the book but an exceptional walk across gentle rolling countryside and past several delightful villages. The final part takes you along The Nicky Line back to Hemel Hempstead. Here you walk through the Old Town before descending through Gadebridge Park back to the car park.

First you walk near the River Gade to Water End having passed the attractive

77

small Gaddesden Hall. A very short road walk brings you to open land through which the clear River Gade glides through before reaching Great Gaddesden. The pub has gone but their is a fine church and an attractive village. Off the route here is a Buddhist compound, you may see some of them in the village. Next you walk through Hoo Wood and onto Jockey End, where again the inn (The Plough) is now a private house. After walking along a track, Dean Lane, you reach one of Hertfordshire's finest buildings, Beechwood House (1644), now a school. Continuing on driveways and paths you reach Markyate with an open inn - The Sun Inn!

Crossing high ground with good views you come to Flamstead with two inns and a fine church. Following paths you cross the M1 and reach your last village, Redbourn, with a fine High Street and several inns. At the southern end of the village you gain The Nicky Line, which you follow all the way back to its end in Hemel Hempstead. Just after you walk through the Old Town, past many inns, before descending back to the car park. As you can see the first half of the walk is "dry", but the second half more than makes up for it!

WALKING INSTRUCTIONS - From the car park head northwards to its entrance at Gadebridge Lane with the bridge (built in 1915) on your right. Turn left to the main Leighton Buzzard Road (A4146). Cross over and turn right and walk along the tarmaced path. There is a right of way on the righthand side of the road - signed - but no path and becomes close to the main road. Follow the path to a road junction with the Marchmont Arms to your right. Keep ahead along the path with the main road on your right, for 1/4 mile to a kissing gate and path sign on your left. Bear slightly right across the field to the next footpath sign and gate. Continue by a fence on your left and onto a gate and drive to Piccotts End Farm on the left. Turn right and left to gain the path, signed Water End. The fenced and hedged path zig zags around the field edges passing an electric sub station well to your right. After about 1/4 mile the path straightens out as you walk beside a hedge on your right. Pass large fish ponds on your right before passing the attractive red bricked, Gaddesden Hall on your right. Soon after use a stile and keep straight ahead with the "Woodlands" on your right. The stiles in this area are well thought out with the top bar hinged allowing you to walk through instead of over. Continue with the hedge/fence on your right to a gate and Willows Lane. Follow it past houses of Water End to Potten End Hill road. Turn right to the A4146 and small area of National Trust land - Ashridge - on your right.

Turn left and walk beside the A4146 road with a lake of the River Gade on your right. In less than 1/4 mile turn left into Nettleden Road; on the right is another piece of Ashridge, National Trust land. Follow the quiet road for less than 1/2 mile to a footpath sign on the right. Turn right and follow the defined path near the lefthand side of the field. To your right is the River Gade and Watercress Beds. Follow the path for nearly 1/2 mile (8 mins.) to a kissing gate on your left at the end of the field. Turn left then right to continue on the path by the hedge on your right to a stile and road with the houses of Great Gaddesden opposite. As you walk well to your right on the valley top is the attractive building of Gaddesden Place. Turn right and left into the village along Church Meadow - No Through Road. In a few yards to your left is the entrance to St. John the Baptist church. Continue along the road passing a former hand pump well on your left. Where the road turns left with a children's play area ahead, keep right to a stile and path sign. Follow the path to a footbridge over the River Gade and onto a stile and the A4146 road.

Go straight across to a track on the right of houses, path signed - Gaddesden Row 1 1/2 miles. Ascend the track and bear left to continue ascending on a defined path to a kissing gate on the southern perimeter of Hoo Wood. Once in the wood keep straight ahead - ignore the path on the right. Follow the path past mostly pine trees. Cross a track and continue on the path to a kissing gate on the northern edge of the wood. Descend beside the hedge before following it right to the end of the field. Turn right and left and continue with the hedge now on your left. Pass a footpath sign and keep ahead to Bradden Lane. Turn right along it passing Hatches Farm and now in Gaddesden Row area. Follow the lane passing Hedgeswood Common on the left and where the lane turns left on your right is a chapel dated 1845. Continue to a road junction and the former inn - The Plough - on your right. You are now in the hamlet of Jockey End. Keep to the lefthand road with a Methodist chapel on the right. Pass the drive to Southing's Farm on the left. Soon after reach Old Ballingdon Farm on your left.

Just after turn right onto Public Byway 73 - road signed Beechwood Lane. In a few yards keep ahead on the track along Dean Lane with Dean Wood on your left. In almost 1/2 mile (10 mins.) reach the wood's end on your left. In a few more yards is a little used right of way on your left. Look for a small cutting leading to a "stile". Over this ascend the field to another "stile" and woodland. The path is little used. Once in the wood aim slightly right and in 50 yards reach a large beech tree. The path line now becomes clear as you can see the school buildings ahead. Aim for the right of them and soon walk past the cricket field on your right, to a car parking area and onto the main driveway to Beechwood House. Turn left along the drive past the most impressive house. If you have trouble on this path you can continue along the

HEMEL HEMPSTEAD, FLAMSTEAD AND THE NICKY LINE - 20 miles - *Map Two.*

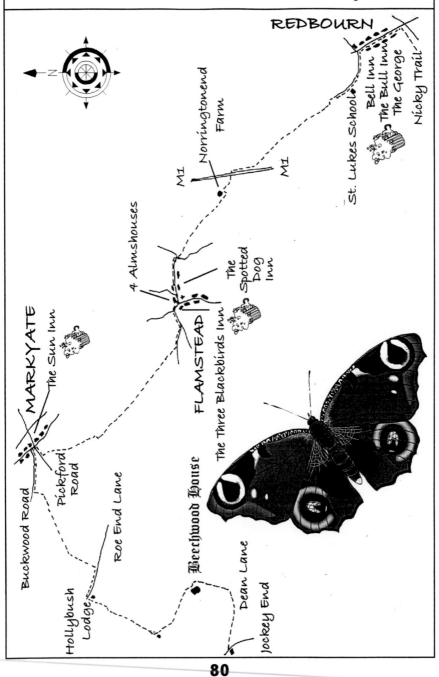

REDBOURN

Nicky Trail

The George
The Bull Inn
Bell Inn

St. Lukes School

Norringtonend Farm

M1

M1

4 Almshouses

The Spotted Dog Inn

FLAMSTEAD

The Three Blackbirds Inn

MARKYATE

The Sun Inn

Buckwood Road

Pickford Road

Roe End Lane

Beechwood House

Dean Lane

Jockey End

Hollybush Lodge

N

Dean Lane track to a road. Here turn left along the field boundary and this, which is also a right of way, leads you to the house drive; where your turn left.

Follow the gravel driveway past the house and onto Kennels Lodge 1/2 mile away - you are also on a part of the Hertfordshire Way. Turn right at the lodge, as footpath signed - ahead is Beechwood Farm - and continue on the drive to Hollybush Lodge, 3/4 mile away. Once there turn right onto a lane and pass Roe End Farm entrance on your left. Soon after with Spring Cottage on your right, turn left at a kissing gate and path signed - Markyate 1 1/2 miles. Keep the hedge on your right to a stile and path sign. Ignore the sharp righthand path, and continue slightly right along the path with a hedge on your right. You descend later to another path, on the edge of Markyate, and turn left to a kissing gate and Buckwood Road. Turn right past the houses of Markyate to the High Street and the Sun Inn. To your left is the attractive main part of the village.

Turn right and right again into Pickford Road. In a short distance opposite house No. 19, turn left onto a hedged path, signed - Flamstead 1 1/2 miles. Ascend the sunken path and soon pass allotments on your right, as you walk beside the hedge on your right. You soon have extensive views to your left and ahead to Flamstead church, your goal. At the end of the field turn right then left to continue along the field edge by the hedge and now a track. Pass a footpath sign on the field corner. Keep ahead across the field on a well defined path. In 3/4 mile reach a kissing gate and path sign. Continue straight ahead with a fence on your left to another kissing gate. Keep ahead to a stile and then along a track to a stile and lane - Friendless Lane. Turn left towards Flamstead. Follow the road left - still Friendless Lane at first before it is named Chapel Road. Continue to a road and turn right to the Three Blackbirds Inn. Just before it turn left along The High Street. Pass four Almshouses on your left before reaching The Spotted Dog on your right; here is the entrance to St. Leonard's Church.

Keep ahead along the road which becomes Singllets Lane and where the road forks, with Delmer End Lane on the right, turn right and left to a kissing gate and path sign. Follow the hedged path to a stile and then keep straight ahead to a bridleway crossed by stiles. Ascend on the faint path aiming for the lefthand corner of a wood. Here turn left then right to continue along the righthand side of the field to a stile and Norringtonend Farm on the left. Turn left to another stile and path sign by the farm drive. Turn right and soon cross the M1 by a bridge. On the other side turn right to walk along a fenced path,

THE NICKY LINE - REDBOURN TO HEMEL HEMPSTEAD - 4 1/2 MILES

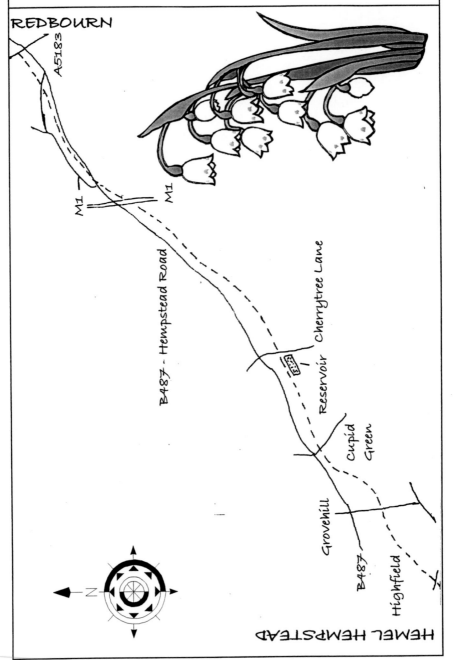

REDBOURN

A5183

M1

M1

B487 - Hempstead Road

Cherrytree Lane

Reservoir

Cupid Green

Grovehill

B487

Highfield

HEMEL HEMPSTEAD

N

first above the motorway and woodland (pine) on the left. Follow the fenced path left at the end to a kissing gate. Continue ahead on the defined path along the field boundary to the end of the field. Turn left and right to continue on the path. Later you have a hedge on your left. Soon pass St. Luke's School on your left as the path becomes tarmaced. Follow it left and right to gain Crouch Hall Lane with the school entrance on the left. Keep ahead along the lane, ignoring all side roads. Reaching Lamb Lane, continue ahead along it to the Redbourn High Street. Turn right and pass shops and the Bell & Skeene Inn; the Bull Inn and The George.

Keep straight ahead through the village and as you approach the railway bridge, turn left up steps to reach The Nicky Line. Turn right and follow the former railway line, 4 1/2 miles, to Hemel Hempstead. First you descend steps and cross a road before continuing on towards the M1. Just before it cross a road and then walk through a tunnel under the M1. Continue on the wooded trail with the Hempstead Road to your right. A mile from the motorway pass under a road bridge and on your left is a reservoir. 1/2 mile later cross a bridge at Cupid Green and another 1/4 mile later. Soon after you reach a road in an Industrial Estate. Follow it left then right to a bend, and on the right the Nicky Trail continues - Hemel Hempstead 1 1/2 miles. The path is now tarmaced. At the next road turn left then right to continue on the trail and soon pass Yew Tree Wood on the left. Nearly 1/2 mile later pass under a road bridge as you gain the Highfield area of the town. In less than 1/2 mile cross another road and descend steps to a park. Turn right along the path - tarmaced - and follow the final section of the trail to Midland Road, with The Midland Inn to the right.

Turn right and follow the road past The Midland to the next road on your right - Alexandra Road. Turn right along this to a cross roads - Queensway. Go straight across into High Street of the Old Town of Hemel Hempstead. Pass the White Hart Inn on the left, then the Old Town Hall and then three inns on the right - The Rose and Crown, Olde Kings Arms and The Bell Inn dated 1603. Continue along High Street to a car park on the left. Turn left and walk through it and on into Gadebridge Park. Cross the park back to the car park, where you began some eight hours ago.

GREAT GADDESDEN - Church dedicated to St. John the Baptist, dates from Norman times. The chancel exterior includes Roman bricks from a former Roman Villa's nearby. There is much of interest inside with may fine monuments to the Halsey and Johnson families. The halsey chapel was built in 1703.

BEECHWOOD HOUSE - The building - Grade I - was built in 1644 for Thomas Saunders. The building includes parts of the earlier house built in 1540 for Sir Richard page. Became a Preparatory School in 1964.

THE HERTFORDSHIRE WAY - 190 mile long circular walk within the boundaries of Hertfordshire, starting and ending at Royston, in the north. Full details of the route and walks along it from the Friends of the Hertfordshire Way - www.fhw.org.uk

FLAMSTEAD - Four Almshouses were given to the village in 1669 by Thomas Saunders the owner of Beechwood House.

Bluebell carpeted woods beside the Nicky Line.

THE NICKY LINE - Former railway line between Hemel Hempstead and harpenden via Redbourn - 7 1/2 miles long.

OLD TOWN, HEMEL HEMPSTEAD -

The Bell Inn, dated 1603, has two poems of the front -

"A truce with thirst
A truce with hunger
They're strong but meat and wine are stronger."
Rabelais. c1500

"God have mercy upon the sinner
who must write with no dinner."
Unknown.

CHIPPERFIELD COMMON & GRAND UNION CANAL - 15 MILES

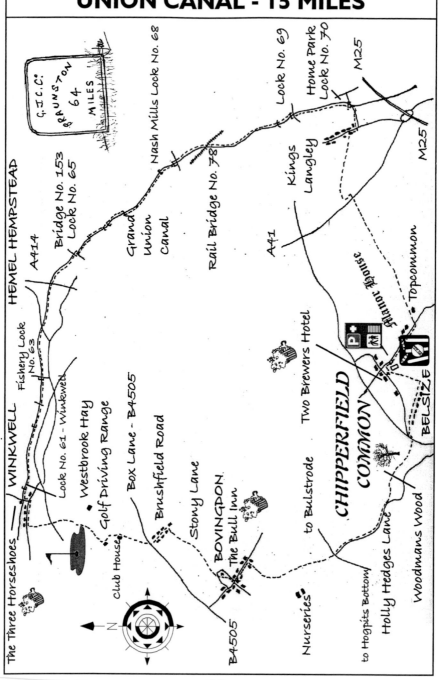

CHIPPERFIELD COMMON AND THE GRAND UNION CANAL
- 15 MILES
- allow 6 hours.

Basic route - Chipperfield Common - Top Common - A41 - Broadfield Farm - A4251 - Home Park Lock No. 70 - Grand Union Canal via Hemel Hempstead to Lock No. 61 - Winkwell Lock No. 61 - Winkwell - Westbrook Hay - Gorsefield Wood - Stoney Lane - Bovingdon - Holly Hedges Lane - Woodman's Wood - Belsize - Chipperfield Common.

Map - O.S. 1:25,000 Explorer Series No. 182 - St. Albans & Hatfield.

Car Park and start - North-East corner of Chipperfield Common. Grid Ref. 182/045015.

Inns - Two Brewers overlooking Chipperfield Common. Ye Olde Red Lion near Lock No. 68. The Paper Mill Inn, Aspley. Fishery Inn near Fishery Lock No. 63. Three Horse Shoes, Winkwell - where you leave the canal. The Bull Inn, and Bell Inn, Bovingdon.

Cafe - Woody's cafe near Aspley Lock No. 67. At Bridge No. 151 on the canal you are close - 8 mins. walk - to central Hemel Hempstead with cafe and inns. Blackwells Cafe, just off the route at Chipperfield Common.

ABOUT THE WALK - You start from an exceptional wooded common, which you see more of on your return path. Crossing undulating fields on good paths you reach the Grand Union Canal on the southern edge of Kings Langley. For the next five miles you follow the canal past numerous locks to Winkwell. You pass close to central Hemel Hempstead and can make a detour to there if you wish; you also walk close to an arm of the canal. From Winkwell you ascend gently past Westbrook Hay and the Little Hay Golf Complex, before gaining an old lane to reach Bovingdon, via its church. Continuing on good paths you reach Holly Hedges Lane before walking through woodland to the village of Belsize. One final short "ascent" along the edge of Chipperfield Common returns you to the start. On the route you follow a section of the Grand Union Canal walk (to Birmingham) and sections of both the Hertfordshire Way and Chilterns Way. During the summer weekends, cricket is played on the Common, opposite the car park.

WALKING INSTRUCTIONS - From the car park beside the cricket green of Chipperfield Common, turn right, away from the village, following a defined path close to the road on your left and just inside woodland. In five minutes on your left can be seen the historic Manor House. After the last house on your left turn left, as path signed to the road. Cross to the drive to Top Common and Hertfordshire Way sign and *"Kings Langley 1 1/2 miles"*. In a short distance the drive turns right; keep ahead to kissing gates as you walk along the lefthand side of the field on a defined path. The path soon becomes a fenced one, as you keep straight ahead to more kissing gates - a feature of this path. Descend to a kissing gate and ascend with a hedge on your right to another kissing gate. The hedge is now on your left to the next kissing gate. Cross the track to Berrybush Farm on the right, and keep straight ahead on a hedged path to a kissing gate. Continue with a hedge on your right, but where it turns right, keep straight ahead on the defined path to a footbridge over the A41. Cross and turn left at the other side, following a defined path which curves right and joins a track. Keep straight ahead along this as you descend to Wayside Farm on the left and Broadfield Farm on the right. Here gain the A425 road.

Turn right and in a few yards left along Station Footpath, which parallels the minor road to the Grand Union Canal. Before the canal and bridge turn right to the road (on your left is Gaywoods Coarse Fishery & Trout Lake) and left to the bridge. Don't cross but keep right and descend past a parking area and steps to the canal. Turn left and pass under the bridge and reach Home Park Lock No. 70. For the next five miles the canal is your companion. First keep the canal on your right and in more than 1/4 mile pass the old Grand Junction Canal Co. milepost - Braunston 68 miles. You will pass four more of these. At the next lock cross to the otherside and continue with the canal on your left. Nearly 1 1/2 miles later, having passed under Rail Bridge No. 78, reach the next lock and cross over to the other side. On your left is the Ye Olde Red Lion Inn. Continue with the canal on your right to Lock No. 68 - Nash Mills. Little over 1/2 mile later at a white bridge, cross the canal again, to continue with it on your left. Pass Stevenson Wharf, Aspley Mill Marina and milepost -

British Waterways

Enjoy the Waterways in Safety

Please Do

- make sure your boat has a valid licence
- navigate with care and consideration and observe the speed limit
- make sure your bicycle has a valid permit
- follow the instructions of British Waterways employees

Please Do Not

- swim or paddle
- fire guns or throw stones
- leave litter or pollute the waterway
- obstruct the towpath
- ride a horse (unless on a designated bridle way) or a motorcycle
- interfere with locks sluices or bridges

This is a summary of British Waterways Bye-laws which can be inspected at any Waterway office. Non-observance may result in prosecution.

66 miles to Braunston. On your left is the Paper Mill Inn, reached by a curving bridge. Pass two more locks before reaching Bridge No. 153. Cross and continue with the canal on your right.

Pass Lock No. 65 and bridge No. 152. More than 1/4 mile later reach bridge No. 151; here you can turn right to the centre of Hemel Hempstead, following the road with a canal arm on the left. Continue to lock No. 64 and milepost - Braunston 65 miles. 3/4 mile late reach the Fishery Inn; Bridge No. 149 and Fishery Lock No. 63. Continue on the towpath with the canal on your right. Pass under bridge No. 148 and pass your last milepost - Braunston 64 miles - see sketch. Nearly 3/4 mile later after passing under Rail Bridge No. 91 reach Winkwell Lock No. 61. Just after reach the road with The Three Horseshoes Inn (since 1535) on the right. Here leave the canal and turn left along the road to the A4251.

Turn right passing the houses of Winkwell for 1/4 mile to the Old Vicarage on the right. Turn left onto a Public Byway and rejoin the Hertfordshire Way. The path/track leads to Memorial Orchard (The Box Moor Trust Estate) on the left, before the bridge over the A41. Cross and reach the golf course - part of the Little Hay Golf Complex. As path signed keep ahead, passing the fourth Green on the right, and gently ascending slightly right, following the arrowed path posts. Pass another green on your left and the 6th. Tee on the right to a footpath sign and seat. To your left is the impressive Westbrook Hay house. Bear right along the edge of the fairway passing woodland on your left. Follow the path left to pass the Driving Range on the right and gain the golf club drive. Follow it right past the Club House on the right, then the 10th. Tee on the left and 1st. Tee on the right. Pass the main car park on the left and soon after, as path signed turn half left to follow a path through Gorsefield Wood to Box Lane.

Turn right then left opposite Little Hay Cottage (1851) and walk along the Private Road - Brushfield Road. At the top opposite Huntsmoor, turn right into Stoney Lane, still on the Hertfordshire Way. Pass Stoney Lane House on the left as the lane becomes a track. Keep straight ahead along it as it becomes a hedged track and follow it to Church Lane, with St. Lawrence Church opposite. Cross the lane and walk through the churchyard past the church on the left to Church Street. Turn right, passing the Bull Inn and left along Chipperfield Road; to your right is the High Street of Bovingdon and The Bell Inn. Follow the road for a 1/4 mile to the second Austins Mead road on the right - path signed - Hertfordshire Way and Chiltern Way. Walk along the road to house No. 52 on the left. Keep ahead now on a path to a kissing gate and fenced path. At the next gate the path bears left by the fence to another gate. Continue with a fence on your left to a kissing gate, and then along the defined path by the hedge on your left. Later the hedge is on your right as you make your way to road T junction.

The Chiltern Way turns right here, but the Hertfordshire Way keeps ahead, as we do, along Holly Hedges Lane. Follow the lane for little over 1/2 mile, passing the house, Hollow Hedge on the left. Where the lane turns sharp right, keep ahead into Woodman's Wood (Forestry Commission); signed - Belsize 3/4 mile. Keep to the wide main path, through the wood, ignoring all others. In 1/4 mile you are walking close to the lefthand side of the wood, before leaving it and walking beside a hedge on your left to the road in Belsize. Turn left and in a few yards opposite Woodmans Lodge, turn right at Windmill Hill (to Bucks Hill). The path - also part of the Hertfordshire Way - is on your right. Ascend the track which becomes a drive along the southern edge of Chipperfield Common. Follow the edge of woodland turning left and right at Mahogany Hall. Pass the houses - White Oaks and The Folly and some 8 mins from the Belsize road, and just after the last house on your right, turn left onto a wide path through the woodland of Chipperfield Common. The path leads directly to the Cricket Pavilion. Turn left around it and on along the cricket field edge to St. Paul's Church (1837). To your left is Blackwells Cafe. Bear right to regain the car park passing the Two Brewers Hotel on the left.

CHIPPERFIELD COMMON - Attractive woodland and large green, where cricket is played. Overlooking it is the Two Brewers Inn and a row of interesting houses, including the historic Manor House. Parts of this house date back to the late 16th. century. The eleven bay wide front was built in 1716.

KINGS LANGLEY - As the name suggests, there was a Royal residence here, used by Henry 3rd. to Richard 2nd. Edward 3rd. fifth son was born here in 1341, and he became the first Duke of York. He lies buried in All saints church and was originally buried in the Dominican Friary, founded by Edward 2nd. in 1308, opposite the Royal Palace.

BOVINGDON - St. Lawrence church was built in 1845. Inside is a 15th. century stone effigy of a knight.

The Grand Union Canal in Hemel Hempstead.

THE GRAND UNION CANAL
- Some brief history notes.

King George I I I in April 1793, gave his assent to an Act of Parliament -

"For making and maintaining a Navigable Canal from Braunston in the County of Northamptonshire to join the River Thames at or near Brentford in the County of Middlesex."

Originally known as the Grand Junction Canal, work began in 1793 with William Jessop of Derbyshire as the Chief Engineer and James Barnes saw to most of the construction work. The most famous section - the Hanwell Flight of six locks - near Brentford was completed in 1794 and raised the canal 53 ft. in 1/3 mile. This flight and the nearby Three Bridges - where the road,canal and railway exactly cross, are now Scheduled Ancient Monuments.

Although sections were opened from 1796 onwards, it wasn't until August 1805 when the canal from Braunston to the River Thames was completely opened. In the meantime the Paddington Branch, from Bull's Bridge to Paddington Basin - 400 yards long by 30 yards wide - was opened on 10th. July 1801. This was a major boost to trade as until then goods were carried on the Thames to the city. There was also a passenger boat service - The Paddington Packet Boat - that ran from Paddington to Uxbridge, and was a great success for many years.

As with all canals the railways brought a decline in use and from the mid 19th. century it was a battle to survive. The Grand Junction fared better than most as it brought goods to and from London. By the 1920's plans were afoot to merge the Warwick, Regent and Grand Junction Canals together and combined they could carry on and make improvements. An Act of Parliament in 1928 allowed the merger to take place on January 1st. 1929. The Regent Canal Company bought the two other canals companies for £801,442. 13p. and the company became known as the Grand Union Canal. New narrow boats were designed which proved a success and run by the Grand Union Canal Carrying Company. In 1948 the canals were nationalised and the Grand Union Canal was one of the last to cease commercial traffic.

As you walk the canal you will see the locks are numbered and named. The bridges are also numbered and sometimes named. There are a few Braunston mile posts scattered around - see sketch - and each London Borough has its own marker.

Grand Union Canal (Grand Junction Canal Co.,) milepost.

The Three Horseshoes Inn, beside the Grand Union Canal at Winkwell.

The Grove (Hotel) and the Grand Union Canal
- see Rickmansworth walk - next page.

RICKMANSWORTH, THE RIVER CHESS AND GRAND UNION CANAL - 15 MILES

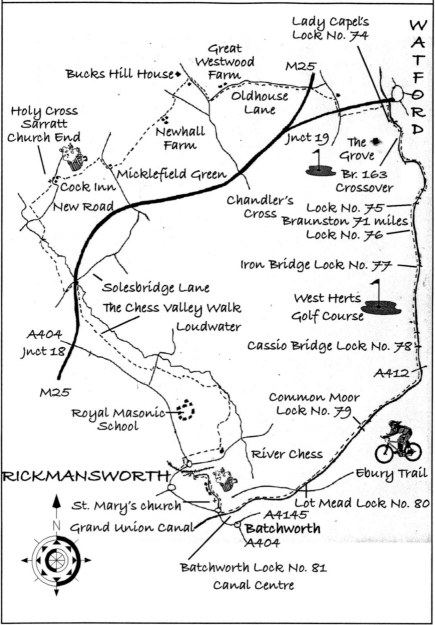

Lady Capel's Lock No. 74

WATFORD

Great Westwood Farm

M25

Bucks Hill House

Oldhouse Lane

Holy Cross Sarratt Church End

Newhall Farm

Jnct 19

The Grove

Br. 163 Crossover

Micklefield Green

Cock Inn

New Road

Chandler's Cross

Lock No. 75
Braunston 71 miles
Lock No. 76

Iron Bridge Lock No. 77

Solesbridge Lane

The Chess Valley Walk

Loudwater

West Herts Golf Course

A404
Jnct 18

Cassio Bridge Lock No. 78

A412

M25

Royal Masonic School

Common Moor Lock No. 79

River Chess

RICKMANSWORTH

Ebury Trail

St. Mary's church

N

Grand Union Canal

Lot Mead Lock No. 80

A4145
Batchworth

A404

Batchworth Lock No. 81
Canal Centre

RICKMANSWORTH,
THE RIVER CHESS
AND THE
GRAND UNION CANAL
- 15 miles
- allow 6 hours.

Basic route - Rickmansworth - The Chess Valley Way - Loudwater Lane - Solesbridge Lane - M25 - River Chess - New Road - Holy Cross Church, (Church End) Sarratt - Micklefield Green - Newhall Farm - High Spring Wood (Bucks Hill) - Great Westwood Farm - Oldhouse Lane - M25 - Clarendon Park - Grand Union Canal - Locks No 74 to 81 - Batchworth Canal Centre - Rickmansworth.

 Map O.S. 1:25,000 Explorer Series No. 172 - Chiltern Hills East.

 Start and end - Rickmansworth Underground Station.

 Inns - The Cock Inn, Church End, Sarratt. The Feathers Inn, Rickmansworth.

 Teas - Beside Batchworth Lock No. 81.

 Ice Cream - Batchworth Canal Centre.

ABOUT THE WALK - A "water" walk in the south western corner of Hertfordshire and what a delight! First you walk beside the River Chess and through the Chess Valley before ascending to Holy Cross church, Sarratt. You have fine views as you ascend and close to the church - about a third of the way round the walk - is the only inn on the walk - The Cock Inn. Following pleasant paths you walk south of Sarratt village before crossing the M25 and gaining the Grand Union Canal. This you follow for five miles back to Batchworth and Rickmansworth, passing several locks. A short walk through the town past an inn returns you to the Underground Station.

97

For those coming by car you can park near Rickmansworth Aquadrome - access from Frogmore Lane - at the northern end of the Colne Valley Park; Grid Ref. 056938. To start the walk follow the Grand Union Canal eastwards to Batchworth Lock, picking up the main route here. See final paragraph for route from Batchworth Lock to Rickmansworth Underground Station. Then start from the beginning of the instructions. Back at Batchworth Lock you retrace your steps back to the car park.

WALKING INSTRUCTIONS - Turn right out of Rickmansworth Station and in a few yards left through the subway beneath the A412. Emerge on the right of the Long Island Exchange and keep ahead. In a few yards bear right and ascend to a footbridge over the A404 road. Cross and keep ahead along an avenue trees on a tarmaced path. You will soon pass a Chess Valley Walk path sign; basically you will follow this walk for the next 5 miles. Pass Rickmansworth Park School on the right and where the drive turns right, keep straight ahead, as path post signed. To your right is the main A412 road and Rickmansworth Roman Catholic church. In a short distance you turn left and follow a fenced path, still on the Chess Valley Walk. First you pass a cricket field on your right before following the path right to the River Chess. Continue on the path, left, by the river on your right. At the top of the slopes on your left is the Royal Masonic School. Soon you come a bridge over the river; do not cross but keep left here on the fenced path as it hugs the perimeter of the school's boundary.

Approaching Loudwater Lane, your first road, keep ahead to it and cross to the right. On the right is the house, Glen Chess. The path is signed - Footpath No. 32 - Chorley Wood Lane. You are still on the Chess Valley Walk. First the path turns left beneath the lane before turning right and becoming a fenced path again. Pass Timberdene on the right and 5 mins. later the path forks; keep right. Pass houses on the left and reach a road. Go straight across - footpath signed - Solesbridge Lane. Follow the path to a drive and keep straight ahead along it to where it turns right to a house. Here on the left is the fenced path which leads to a stile and on beneath the M25 road. In nearly 1/2 mile reach Solesbridge Lane with Solesbridge Mill Water gardens on the right. Turn left and cross the motorway.

Before the first house on the right, turn right, as path signed - Sarratt Green Mill 1 mile; you are still on the Chess Valley Walk. The path soon becomes a drive as you walk close to the Chorleywood House Estate - you pass a historical information board on your left. Soon after the board the drive bears right to a mill. Here keep ahead on a track in woodland and reach a kissing gate. Bear

98

right to a footbridge over the River Chess and follow the path along the field edge and turn left by the hedge to gain a kissing gate and New Road. Go straight across and continue on a drive with the river and Sarratt Mill House to your left. Reach house No. 2 and leave the Chess Valley walk and turn right and keep the fence on your left as you ascend to a stile with views behind of the Chess Valley and Chenies. Continue to a kissing gate and Holy Cross church at Church End, Sarratt.

Turn right along Church Lane, passing six almshouses built in 1821 by M. Ralph Desy of Sarratt Hall. Just after pass The Cock Inn and turn right through the car park - path signed Micklefield Green 3/4 mile. Cross to the far lefthand corner and a stile. Follow the path to a stile and onto another before bearing left to continue by the hedge on your left to a road. Before the road turn right and continue by the hedge, with the road on your left, for 200 yards to a stile on your left and path sign - Bucks Hill 1 mile. Cross the road with Woodwalks Cottage on the left. Follow the path to a stile and on along the righthand side of the field to another and hedged track. Turn left and follow the track for more than 1/2 mile to a large barn of Newhall Farm. Keep straight ahead, as path signed, and cross the farm drive and walk along the path on the left of the barn. Beyond keep to the righthand side of the field on the defined path to a valley side; ahead can be seen Bucks Hill House. Descend the path to Bottom Lane and stile. Turn left and in a few yards right - path signed Bucks Hill 1/2 mile. Ascend past beech trees of High Spring Wood to a road with Bucks Hill House on the left and Petherick Pasture on the right.

Turn right along the road and in more than 1/4 mile turn left along Oldhouse Lane. Pass Great Westwood Farm on your left and descend the lane to woodland. Here there is a path on the right but it is not defined in the wood. Continue on the lane and ascend steeply, briefly, before crossing the M25. Immediately afterwards turn right, as path signed - No. 47 - Langleybury Lane 394 yards. Descend steps and reach a stile and then continue by the fence on the right with woodland on the left. The path can be overgrown in places in the summer. Gain the lane with South Lodge opposite. Turn right and cross the Watford link of the M25. Just after turn left to a gate and track - path signed Public Restricted Byway 71 - Hempstead Road 3/4 mile. Pass woodland on your right then Clarendon Park Farm. Keep straight ahead and as you approach the Grand Union Canal the path forks. Keep left to gain the canal towpath close to the M25 bridge.

Turn right and for the next 5 miles you walk beside the canal to Batchworth Lock No. 81 and the Batchworth Canal Centre. First you reach Lady Capel's

Lock No 74 and soon after a crossover bridge, No. 163. Cross the canal and continue now the canal on your right. To your right is The Grove (Hotel) and golf course. Continue to Grove Mill Lane and bridge no. 165. Continue with the canal on the right to bridge No. 166. Here you cross the canal again and for the remainder of the walk the canal is on your left. Pass locks No. 75 and 76 and canal milepost - Braunston 71 miles. 3/4 mile later gain Iron Bridge Lock No. 77. The bridge closeby No. 167 has fine examples of the rope grooves made by the horse ropes pulling the narrowboats. A mile later pass Cassio Bridge Lock No. 78 - Rickmansworth is 3 miles from here! Pass P & S Marina on the left and the canal turns right and in nearly another mile reaches Common Moor Lock No. 79.

Continue on the towpath and in another mile reach Lot Mead Lock No. 80. and the Ebury Way. Just after is your final milepost - Braunston 74 miles. The canal curves right and left to Batchworth Lock No. 81. Here is a Cafe cabin and Canal Centre. Leave the canal here and gain the main road - A404. Turn right and keep right at the roundabout to walk into the town centre. Pass St, Mary's church on your left - you can walk through the churchyard and cut the road corner off. Continue past The Feathers Inn and turn left along High Street. Partway along turn right along Station Road and at the top turn left to the station.

The Chess Valley Way logo and path sign.

RICKMANSWORTH - From Saxon times the town has grown in importance being at the confluence of three rivers - Chess, Glade and Colne. In 1542 the town was granted a Royal Charter. With the canal being built here in 1797 businesses grew with a brewery and five paper mills. William Penn lived here in Basing House, now the Three Rivers Museum. The state of Pennsylvania , USA, is named after him.

St. Mary the Virgin church - Dates from the 12th. century and belonged to the Abbot of St. Albans. Although altered over the centuries it was rebuilt in 1826, at a cost of £6,000 and could accommodate 2,000 worshippers. The tower dates from 1630. There are several fine stained glass windows and memorials. One is to Sir Thomas Fotherley who died in 1649. He was a Privy Counsellor to Charles 2nd. Another is the Monmouth Memorial.

HOLY CROSS CHURCH, CHURCH END, SARRATT - A delightful church dating back to the 12th. century and mostly made from flint and some Roman bricks can be seen. The bell tower is 15th. century with three bells made at the Whitechapel Bell Foundry, (London). The Jacobean pulpit was made c1606. On the wall opposite can be seen part of a 14th. century wall painting. The chancel has several fine monuments including the 17th. century Kingsley Memorial and another to a person who drowned.

The paths in the Parish of Sarratt have their own logo
- what a good idea; individuality is the spice of life!

GRAND UNION CANAL - 300 miles of canal from the River Thames to near Daventry where it splits into two, with one branch going to Leicester and the other to Birmingham. The London (Little Venice) to Birmingham (Gas Street Basin) section is a signed path of 145 miles. There are several canal arms to places such as Slough, Aylesbury and Northampton. The canal dating from the 1790's was part of several independent canals, which all linked together. In 1929 they were finally brought together as one unit aptly known as the Grand Union Canal.

THE GROVE - Impressive early 18th. century brick building. The stucco bridge over the Grand Union Canal was made about 1800.

EBURY WAY - 3 1/2 mile cycleway along the former railway line, linking Rickmansworth and Watford. The railway line was built by Lord Ebury in 1862 and was closed in 1981.

BATCHWORTH CANAL CENTRE - Interesting display of the history of the canal in this area; well worth a visit. Closeby is the River Chess Lock. A popular Canal Festival is held here each May. www.rwt.org.uk

Canal Crossover Bridge No. 163.

The tranquil Grand Union Canal and lock.

Cassiobury Park Lock No. 76 and cottage.

WALK RECORD CHART

Date walked -

Around Welwyn Garden City - 19 miles ....

Norton Bury, Ashwell, Caldecote & Stotfold - 15 miles ....

Nomansland, Old Railways and Rivers - 18 miles ....

Whitwell, Knebworth, Preston, King's Walden

and St. Paul's Walden - 18 miles..

Ayot St. Lawrence and the River Lee - 15 miles ....

"Town & Country" - Stanmore & River Colne - 20 miles.................

Hemel Hempstead, Flamstead and the Nicky Line - 20 miles ....

Chipperfield Common and Grand Union Canal - 15 miles ....

Rickmansworth, The River Chess

and Grand Union Canal - 15 miles ....

THE JOHN MERRILL WALK BADGE

Complete six walks in this book and get the above special embroidered badge and signed certificate. Badges are Blue cloth with lettering and hiker embroidered in four colours.

BADGE ORDER FORM

Date walks completed...

NAME ....

ADDRESS ....

....

Price: £5.00 each including postage, packing, VAT and signed completion certificate. Amount enclosed (Payable to The John Merrill Foundation).

Happy Walking T Shirt - yellow - £8.95 inc. postage - state size required.

From: The John Merrill Foundation,
32, Holmesdale, Waltham Cross,
Hertsfordshire, EN8 8QY

Tel/Fax 01992 - 762776
e-mail - marathonhiker@aol.com

Order on line - www.johnmerrillwalkguides.com

********** YOU MAY PHOTOCOPY THIS FORM   **********

Companion guide -
Nine long walks in Eastern Hertfordshire - 15 to 20 miles long.

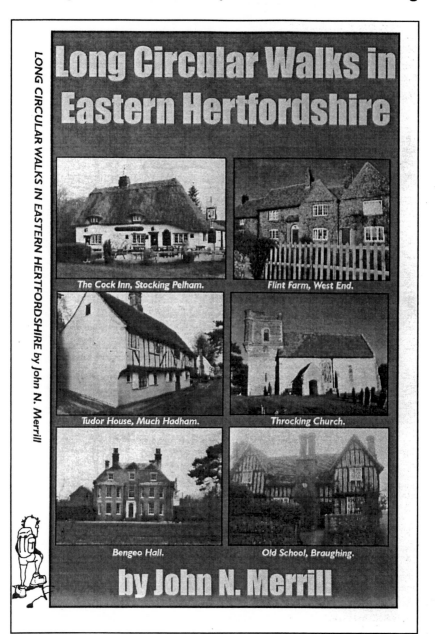

LONG CIRCULAR WALKS IN EASTERN HERTFORDSHIRE by John N. Merrill

Long Circular Walks in Eastern Hertfordshire

The Cock Inn, Stocking Pelham.

Flint Farm, West End.

Tudor House, Much Hadham.

Throcking Church.

Bengeo Hall.

Old School, Braughing.

by John N. Merrill

OTHER NORTH LONDON WALK BOOKS
by JOHN N. MERRILL

SHORT CIRCULAR WALKS ON THE RIVER LEE NAVIGATION - Northern Volume -
Ponder's End - Hertford. 64 pages, 23 photographs, 10 detailed maps and walks. History notes.
- ISBN 1-903627-68-0 @ £7.95

WALKING THE RIVER LEE NAVIGATION - VOL 1 & 2.

SHORT CIRCULAR WALKS ON THE NEW RIVER & SOUTH EAST HERTFORDSHIRE
11 walks - 5 to 10 miles long between Waltham Cross and Hertford; many on the New River. New revised and enlarged edition 68 pages, 24 photographs , 13 detailed maps. History notes.
ISBN 1-903627-69-9 @ £7.95

SHORT CIRCULAR WALKS IN EPPING FOREST
10 circular walks 6 to 18 miles long. Combined they explore the whole forest and its surrounding area. 68 pages. 12 maps. 30 photographs. History notes.
ISBN 1-903627-72-9 @ £7.95

LONG CIRCULAR WALKS IN EASTERN HERTFORDSHIRE
9 walks - 15 to 20 miles long. Beautiful unspoilt walking in rolling countryside full of historical interest. £9.95
ISBN 978-0-9553691-7-9

LONG CIRCULAR WALKS IN WESTERN HERTFORDSHIRE
- 9 long walks - 15 to 20 miles.. 112 pages. Wire bound. 55 photographs. 20detailed maps. £9.95 ISBN 978-0-955651113

SHORT CIRCULAR WALKS AROUND HERTFORD.
3 historical Town walks and four country walks.
ISBN 978-0-9556511-7-5 £9.95

SHORT CIRCULAR WALKS ON THE RIVER STORT NAVIGATION
8 circular walks; 1 End to End walk. Full history and photographic study of this peaceful waterway. 92 pages. 68 photographs. 12 maps. ISBN 1-903627- 73-7 £9.95

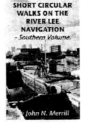

SHORT CIRCULAR WALKS ON THE RIVER LEE NAVIGATION - Southern Volume -
Limehouse basin to Hackney Marsh. 5 walks on the Regent Canal, Hertford Union and Limehouse Cut. Including Three Mills and its rivers. The guide also details a 28 mile End to End walk along the Navigation. 68 pages. 10 maps, 30 photographs.
ISBn 1-903627-74-5 £7.95

EPPING FOREST CHALLENGE WALK - 21 MILES.
Starts and ends at Waltham Abbey and takes in the whole forest. 44 pages. 6 maps. 10 photos £5.95
ISBN 978-0-9553691-0-0

"St. ALBANS WAY" - 26 mile Pilgrims walk from Waltham Abbey to St. Alban's Cathedral.
£5.95
ISBN 978-0-9553691-3-1

NORTH LONDON - THE THREE BOROUGH CHALLENGE WALK - 21 MILES
A walk linking together the three boroughs of Enfield, Barnet and Haringey.
A magnificent countryside walk. Certificate for the successful.
A5. 40 pages. Full colour book.
ISBN 978-0-9556511-9-9
£5.95

OTHER JOHN MERRILL WALK BOOKS

CIRCULAR WALK GUIDES -
SHORT CIRCULAR WALKS IN THE PEAK DISTRICT - VOL. 1,2, 3 AND 9
CIRCULAR WALKS IN WESTERN PEAKLAND
SHORT CIRCULAR WALKS IN THE STAFFORDSHIRE MOORLANDS
SHORT CIRCULAR WALKS - TOWNS & VILLAGES OF THE PEAK DISTRICT
SHORT CIRCULAR WALKS AROUND MATLOCK
SHORT CIRCULAR WALKS IN "PEAK PRACTICE COUNTRY."
SHORT CIRCULAR WALKS IN THE DUKERIES
SHORT CIRCULAR WALKS IN SOUTH YORKSHIRE
SHORT CIRCULAR WALKS IN SOUTH DERBYSHIRE
SHORT CIRCULAR WALKS AROUND BUXTON
SHORT CIRCULAR WALKS AROUND WIRKSWORTH
SHORT CIRCULAR WALKS IN THE HOPE VALLEY
40 SHORT CIRCULAR WALKS IN THE PEAK DISTRICT
CIRCULAR WALKS ON KINDER & BLEAKLOW
SHORT CIRCULAR WALKS IN SOUTH NOTTINGHAMSHIRE
SHORT CIRCULAR WALKS IN CHESHIRE
SHORT CIRCULAR WALKS IN WEST YORKSHIRE
WHITE PEAK DISTRICT AIRCRAFT WRECKS
CIRCULAR WALKS IN THE DERBYSHIRE DALES
SHORT CIRCULAR WALKS FROM BAKEWELL
SHORT CIRCULAR WALKS IN LATHKILL DALE
CIRCULAR WALKS IN THE WHITE PEAK
SHORT CIRCULAR WALKS IN EAST DEVON
SHORT CIRCULAR WALKS AROUND HARROGATE
SHORT CIRCULAR WALKS IN CHARNWOOD FOREST
SHORT CIRCULAR WALKS AROUND CHESTERFIELD
SHORT CIRCULAR WALKS IN THE YORKS DALES - VOL 1 - SOUTHERN AREA.
SHORT CIRCULAR WALKS IN THE AMBER VALLEY (DERBYSHIRE)
SHORT CIRCULAR WALKS IN THE LAKE DISTRICT
SHORT CIRCULAR WALKS IN THE NORTH YORKSHIRE MOORS
SHORT CIRCULAR WALKS IN EAST STAFFORDSHIRE
LONG CIRCULAR WALKS IN THE PEAK DISTRICT - VOL.1, 2 , 3, 4 AND 5.
DARK PEAK AIRCRAFT WRECK WALKS
LONG CIRCULAR WALKS IN THE STAFFORDSHIRE MOORLANDS
LONG CIRCULAR WALKS IN CHESHIRE
WALKING THE TISSINGTON TRAIL
WALKING THE HIGH PEAK TRAIL
WALKING THE MONSAL TRAIL & SETT VALLEY TRAILS
PEAK DISTRICT WALKING - TEN "TEN MILER'S" - VOL ONE AND TWO
CLIMB THE PEAKS OF THE PEAK DISTRICT
PEAK DISTRICT WALK A MONTH VOLS ONE, TWO, THREE, FOUR, FIVE & SIX
TRAIN TO WALK VOL. ONE - THE HOPE VALLEY LINE
DERBYSHIRE LOST VILLAGE WALKS -VOL ONE AND TWO.
CIRCULAR WALKS IN DOVEDALE AND THE MANIFOLD VALLEY
CIRCULAR WALKS AROUND GLOSSOP
WALKING THE LONGDENDALE TRAIL
WALKING THE UPPER DON TRAIL
SHORT CIRCULAR WALKS IN CANNOCK CHASE
CIRCULAR WALKS IN THE DERWENT VALLEY
WALKING THE TRAILS OF NORTH-EAST DERBYSHIRE
WALKING THE PENNINE BRIDLEWAY & CIRCULAR WALKS
SHORT CIRCULAR WALKS ON THE NEW RIVER & SOUTH-EAST HERTFORDSHIRE
SHORT CIRCULAR WALKS IN EPPING FOREST
WALKING THE STREETS OF LONDON
LONG CIRCULAR WALKS IN EASTERN HERTFORDSHIRE
LONG CIRCULAR WALKS IN WESTERN HERTFORDSHIRE
WALKS IN THE LONDON BOROUGH OF ENFIELD
WALKS IN THE LONDON BOROUGH OF BARNET
WALKS IN THE LONDON BOROUGH OF HARINGEY
WALK IN THE LONDON BOROUGH OF WALTHAM FOREST
SHORT CIRCULAR WALKS AROUND HERTFORD
THE BIG WALKS OF LONDON

CANAL WALKS -
VOL 1 - DERBYSHIRE & NOTTINGHAMSHIRE
VOL 2 - CHESHIRE & STAFFORDSHIRE
VOL 3 - STAFFORDSHIRE
VOL 4 - THE CHESHIRE RING
VOL 5 - THE GRANTHAM CANAL
VOL 6 - SOUTH YORKSHIRE
VOL 7 - THE TRENT & MERSEY CANAL
VOL 8 - WALKING THE DERBY CANAL RING
VOL 9 - WALKING THE LLANGOLLEN CANAL
VOL 10 - CIRCULAR WALKS ON THE CHESTERFIELD CANAL
VOL 11 - CIRCULAR WALKS ON THE CROMFORD CANAL
VOL.13 - SHORT CIRCULAR WALKS ON THE RIVER LEE NAVIGATION -VOL. 1 - NORTH
VOL. 14 - SHORT CIRCULAR WALKS ON THE RIVER STORT NAVIGATION
VOL.15 - SHORT CIRCULAR WALKS ON THE RIVER LEE NAVIGATION - VOL. 2 - SOUTH
VOL. 16 - WALKING THE CANALS OF LONDON
VOL 17 - WALKING THE RIVER LEE NAVIGATION
VOL. 20 - SHORT CIRCULAR WALKS IN THE COLNE VALLEY

JOHN MERRILL DAY CHALLENGE WALKS -
WHITE PEAK CHALLENGE WALK
THE HAPPY HIKER - WHITE PEAK - CHALLENGE WALK No.2
DARK PEAK CHALLENGE WALK
PEAK DISTRICT END TO END WALKS
STAFFORDSHIRE MOORLANDS CHALLENGE WALK

For a free complete catalogue of John Merrill walk Guides send a SAE to The John Merrill Foundation

**Visit our website -
www.walkinglondon.org**

THE LITTLE JOHN CHALLENGE WALK
YORKSHIRE DALES CHALLENGE WALK
NORTH YORKSHIRE MOORS CHALLENGE WALK
LAKELAND CHALLENGE WALK
THE RUTLAND WATER CHALLENGE WALK
MALVERN HILLS CHALLENGE WALK
THE SALTER'S WAY
THE SNOWDON CHALLENGE
CHARNWOOD FOREST CHALLENGE WALK
THREE COUNTIES CHALLENGE WALK (Peak District).
CAL-DER-WENT WALK by Geoffrey Carr,
THE QUANTOCK WAY
BELVOIR WITCHES CHALLENGE WALK
THE CARNEDDAU CHALLENGE WALK
THE SWEET PEA CHALLENGE WALK
THE LINCOLNSHIRE WOLDS - BLACK DEATH - CHALLENGE WALK
JENNIFER'S CHALLENGE WALK
THE EPPING FOREST CHALLENGE WALK
THE THREE BOROUGH CHALLENGE WALK - NORTH LONDON

INSTRUCTION & RECORD -
HIKE TO BE FIT.....STROLLING WITH JOHN
THE JOHN MERRILL WALK RECORD BOOK
HIKE THE WORLD - John Merrill's guide to walking & Backpacking.

MULTIPLE DAY WALKS -
THE RIVERS'S WAY
PEAK DISTRICT: HIGH LEVEL ROUTE
PEAK DISTRICT MARATHONS
THE LIMEY WAY
THE PEAKLAND WAY
COMPO'S WAY by Alan Hiley
THE BRIGHTON WAY by Norman Willis

**Visit our website -
www.pilgrimways.co.uk**

THE PILGRIM WALKS SERIES -
THE WALSINGHAM WAY - ELY TO WALSINGHAM - 72 MILES
THE WALSINGHAM WAY - Kings Lynn to Walsingham - 35 miles
TURN LEFT AT GRANJA DE LA MORERUELA - 700 MILES
NORTH TO SANTIAGO DE COMPOSTELA, VIA FATIMA - 650 MILES
St. OLAV'S WAY - Oslo to Trondheim - 400 miles
St. WINEFRIDE'S WAY - St. Asaph to Holywell
St. ALBANS WAY - Waltham Abbey to St. Albans - 26 miles
St. KENELM TRAIL by John Price - Clent Hills to Winchcombe - 60 miles
DERBYSHIRE PILGRIMAGES
LONDON TO CANTERBURY- 83 MILES

COAST WALKS & NATIONAL TRAILS -
ISLE OF WIGHT COAST PATH
PEMBROKESHIRE COAST PATH
THE CLEVELAND WAY
WALKING ANGELSEY'S COASTLINE.
WALKING THE COASTLINE OF THE CHANNEL ISLANDS
THE ISLE OF MAN COASTAL PATH - *"The Way of the Gull."*
A WALK AROUND HAYLING ISLAND
A WALK AROUND THE ISLE OF SHEPPEY

For a free
complete
catalogue of
John Merrill
walk Guides
send a SAE to
The John Merrill
Foundation

DERBYSHIRE & PEAK DISTRICT HISTORICAL GUIDES -
A TO Z GUIDE OF THE PEAK DISTRICT
DERBYSHIRE INNS - AN A TO Z GUIDE
HALLS AND CASTLES OF THE PEAK DISTRICT & DERBYSHIRE
TOURING THE PEAK DISTRICT & DERBYSHIRE BY CAR
DERBYSHIRE FOLKLORE
PUNISHMENT IN DERBYSHIRE
CUSTOMS OF THE PEAK DISTRICT & DERBYSHIRE
WINSTER - A SOUVENIR GUIDE
ARKWRIGHT OF CROMFORD
LEGENDS OF DERBYSHIRE
DERBYSHIRE FACTS & RECORDS
TALES FROM THE MINES by Geoffrey Carr
PEAK DISTRICT PLACE NAMES by Martin Spray
DERBYSHIRE THROUGH THE AGES - Vol 1 -DERBYSHIRE IN PREHISTORIC TIMES
SIR JOSEPH PAXTON
FLORENCE NIGHTINGALE
JOHN SMEDLEY
BONNIE PRINCE CHARLIE & 20 MILE WALK.
THE STORY OF THE EARLS AND DUKES OF DEVONSHIRE

JOHN MERRILL'S MAJOR WALKS -
TURN RIGHT AT LAND'S END
WITH MUSTARD ON MY BACK
TURN RIGHT AT DEATH VALLEY
EMERALD COAST WALK
I CHOSE TO WALK - Why I walk etc.
A WALK IN OHIO - 1,310 miles around the Buckeye Trail.

**Visit our website -
www.johnmerrillwalkguides.com**

SKETCH BOOKS -
SKETCHES OF THE PEAK DISTRICT

COLOUR BOOK:-
THE PEAK DISTRICT.......something to remember her by.

OVERSEAS GUIDES -
HIKING IN NEW MEXICO - Vol I - The Sandia and Manzano Mountains.
Vol 2 - Hiking "Billy the Kid" Country. Vol 4 - N.W. area - " Hiking Indian Country."
"WALKING IN DRACULA COUNTRY" - Romania.
WALKING THE TRAILS OF THE HONG KONG ISLANDS.

VISITOR GUIDES - MATLOCK . BAKEWELL. ASHBOURNE.